The Art of African Textiles: Technology, Tradition and Lurex

(overleaf) ☛
Wax print cotton textile
'Flashlights' design
Printed by Faso Fani, Burkina Faso, 1990s
The Newark Museum, New Jersey

THE ART OF
AFRICAN TEXTILES
TECHNOLOGY, TRADITION AND LUREX

John Picton

Rayda Becker ✹ Pauline Duponchel ✹ Jackie Guille
Elizabeth Harney ✹ David Heathcote ✹ Julia Hilger ✹ Atta Kwami
Pat Oyelola ✹ Simon Peers

Barbican Art Gallery
Lund Humphries Publishers
London

CONTENTS

Cotton textile (*adanudo*)
Ewe, Ghana
Early 20th century
Collection Peter Adler

FOREWORD

Say it to the one who knows it all
You might have learnt something, but many things have slipped you by!
[Abu Nawas]
Diwan Abu Nawas, Dar Hilal, Beirut, 1986, p.10
Translated by Abdullah al-Udhari

🌍 At the entrance to this exhibition hangs an appliqué made earlier this year, just after Ramadan, by Salah El Din M. El Ozy in the *khayameyeen*, the tent-makers' quarter, of Cairo. It has been cut and sewn by hand from factory-woven cloth in the manner that the artist has followed over the past fifty years or so. At the close of the exhibition is a newly created installation by the Nigeria-born, London-based artist Yinka Shonibare. His Victorian-style costumes are made of wax print cotton textiles produced in Europe for Africa: a comment on imperialism, African history and cultural identity. These two pieces, contrasting as they are and different again from the woven, dyed and printed cloths shown in the body of the exhibition, give an indication of the many ways in which textiles in Africa have been made and used and how they have changed and developed through the course of this century. The exhibition is certainly about such diversity but, above all, it is concerned with the tremendous importance that textiles have had, and continue to have, within the visual arts of Africa.

🌍 *The Art of African Textiles : Technology, Tradition and Lurex* began with a telephone call from Clementine Deliss at the time that she was forming *Africa 95*, the season of arts events of which this exhibition is a part. She was aware that the gallery was considering making an exhibition of contemporary African art of some kind, based on initial research in North Africa supported by Visiting Arts. It became clear during our first meeting that *Africa 95* might well create the opportunity we were looking for, and our approach has been coloured by *Africa 95*'s regard for the contemporary situation and the entire continent of Africa (even though the initial plans we discussed have changed considerably). Indeed, it was Clementine Deliss who, a few years previously, had drawn John Picton's attention to the emblematic interests of West African fancy prints, leading to their inclusion here.

🌍 Not long afterwards, John Hoole, Curator of Barbican Art Gallery, happened to visit Japan in relation to a quite different project (although, it must be said, one in which the cross-fertilisation of ideas between continents and cultures was very much to the fore). While there, he saw the version of the exhibition of African textiles organised by John Mack and Christopher Spring of the Museum of Mankind, London, which built upon the earlier exhibition (1979) curated by John Picton and John Mack at the Museum of Mankind. That visit gave impetus to the present exhibition which, in a sense, is a development from and commentary on those earlier explorations.

🌍 As it has evolved, the exhibition has undoubtedly been both more complex and more fascinating than we had ever imagined. It has emerged out of a desire to show that textiles in Africa have always changed, and to recognise the creativity with which new methods and materials are absorbed, new concepts devised, and

ready-made fabrics reworked. John Picton, Reader in African Art, School of Oriental and African Studies, University of London, has played a central role. Not only his expertise, but also his delight in the fact that everything may be questioned and that things are rarely what they seem, have directed the development of the exhibition and catalogue. We quickly realised that each element was a story in itself, worthy of a complete exhibition, whether it be the *niombo* (fabric coffins made of imported blankets) of Sundi-Kongo; the Asante and Ewe cloths of Ghana; or factory-printed textiles. With such a vast array of material to choose from, it was evident that we could not be comprehensive. The Museum of Mankind, London, will be showing concurrently exhibitions of textiles from North Africa (*Display and Modesty*), and Ethiopia (*Secular and Sacred*), and so we have limited the representation of those regions within our own exhibition. Older examples of Egyptian appliqué hangings can be found there, and there are also resonances within other exhibitions that are part of *Africa 95*: the Royal Academy's *Africa : The Art of a Continent*; *Seven Stories about Modern Art in Africa* at Whitechapel Art Gallery, London; *Siyawela : Contemporary Art from South Africa* at the Gas Hall Birmingham; and, not least, the Barbican Centre's Concourse Gallery exhibition, *Signs , Traces and Calligraphy*.

🌍 In reflecting upon the path the exhibition has taken, the inscription that our appliqué entrance bears (see above) now seems of particular relevance. Taken from the writings of Abu Nawas, it provides an apt reminder that, inevitably, there are aspects of significance which we have omitted. Yet it also gives an indication of what we hope the exhibition achieves: that it challenges assumptions about the place and nature of textiles in Africa, and, importantly, points towards the numerous questions still to be asked and the many tales yet to be told. Moreover, the three terms of the sub-title of the exhibition and catalogue (taken from John Picton's paper published by the Smithsonian Institution Press, Washington DC, 1992) are particularly emblematic of these questions and tales, even while we recognise that there is far more to twentieth-century development than lurex.

🌍 Barbican Art Gallery and John Picton wish to thank the many people who have been involved during the making of the exhibition. Research into current textile production was undertaken specially for us by Jackie Guille (South Africa, Zambia, Zimbabwe), Julia Hilger (Kenya, Tanzania), Atta Kwami (Ghana), and Pat Oyelola (Nigeria), each of whom has contributed to this catalogue, as have Rayda Becker, Pauline Duponchel, Elizabeth Harney, David Heathcote and Simon Peers. Others have also been generous in making details of their own research available to us: Brian Anderton, Lisa Aronson, Kathleen Bickford, Duncan Clarke and Carolyn Keyes-Adenaike.

🦋 We have been fortunate in receiving a great deal of help and advice within Europe and in North America. In Britain, we are particularly grateful to Philip Poole, Gail Russell, Marilyn Hoyle and Margaret Hickon, staff of A.Brunnschweiler & Co., for their hospitality and kind cooperation throughout; also to John Carmichael, Elsbeth Court, Julia Ellis, Julie Hudson, Dale Idiens, Rose Issa, Macolm McLeod, John Mack, Keith Nicklin, Susan Picton, Christopher Spring, and Lou Taylor; in France, Claude Ardouin, Marine Biras, Michèle Coquet, Jocelyn Etienne-Nugue, Etienne Féau, Karen Petrossian, Josette Rivallain, Dominique Taffin, and in Germany, Edward Norris. In the Netherlands, we are particularly grateful to F. van Rood and J.Verhof of Vlisco bv for their hospitality and kind cooperation, and to Bea Brommer, Annemieke Hogervorst and Pauline Burmann for their generous help. In Canada and the USA we thank those who have offered advice from the early stages: Mary Jo Arnoldi, Marion John, Sarah Kennington, Doran H. Ross, Anne M. Spencer, and Roslyn A. Walker.

🦋 We are particularly indebted to the artists, scholars and galleries, museums and other organisations in Africa itself, without whom it would have been impossible to make the exhibition. Many have given much of their time and support, offering advice and helping with the organisation of research visits, including: in Egypt, Basma El-Husseiny of the British Council, who assisted in the coordination and gave enthusiastic support; and in Ghana, Tom Cowin, Director of the British Council, and staff of the University of Science and Technology (UST), Kumasi. In Mali, Paul and Tessa Gueye offered great kindness and assistance, and we are also grateful to M.D. Diouma, Ministry of Culture and Arts, and particularly to Souleyman Sissouma and staff of the Institut National des Arts, who contributed to the research and gave great support. Similarly we thank Samuel Sidibé and staff of the Musée National including Baba Fallo Keita, Abdoulay Konate and M.Sogodogo. Our thanks also go to Fambourgouri Diane and staff of ITEMA and Pauline Duponchel. In Nigeria, we acknowledge the generous assistance of Afprint and thank the National Commission for Museums and Monuments of Nigeria for permission to reproduce photographs by John Picton from 1968 to 1969. We were given great assistance in Senegal by Nikolai Cisse, Oumou Sy, Moustapha Tambadou and the Ministry of Culture, Papa Ibra Tall and the Manufactures Sénégalaises des Arts Décoratifs. In South Africa we were assisted by Marilyn Martin, Emma Bedford and Carole Kauffman of the National Gallery, Cape Town; Rochelle Keane, Nessa Leibhammey, and Lesley Spiro of Johannesburg Art Gallery; Bruce Campbell-Smith, Patricia Davison, Linda Givon, Juliette Leeb-du Toit, Napo Makoena, Carey May, Ivor Powell, Kim Sacks, Sydney Selepe and Gavin Younge, and we offer especial thanks to Rayda Becker, University of the Witwatersrand, Johannesburg, who worked with us on the selection of the South African section of the exhibition. We are grateful in Zambia to staff of Kafue Textiles and to Shoba Ponnappa of the British Council for assisting Jackie Guille in her research; and in Zimbabwe to Gerry Eyres of the British Council, Murray McCartney and Irene Staunton, Ilse Noy (formerly of Cold Comfort Farm), Stephen Williams, and Ray Woolley of David Whitehead Textiles Ltd. In relation to her research in Kenya and Tanzania we would like to thank on behalf of Julia Hilger: Fatma Abdullah, Ali Shaaban Abdullah and family, Crispin Ellis, Hans and Sybille Hilger, Mr Kaderdina and family, staff of Rift Valley Textiles, Tania Tribe, Zainab Yahya, as well as the people of Paje, Zanzibar.

🦋 The exhibition has been generously supported by our sponsors Barclays (Ghana), Barclays (Kenya), Barclays (Zimbabwe) and Barclays (Zambia). Their help has been of special importance for this exhibition, enabling new research to be undertaken, as has that of the Arts Council of England. We acknowledge with thanks the support given to John Picton's research in Nigeria by the National Commission for Museums and Monuments of Nigeria (NCMM), the British Academy and the School of Oriental and African Studies, London; as well as the support of the British Council, Ghana, which has enabled Atta Kwami to visit London.

🦋 Africa 95 have continued to support our exhibition enthusiastically, especially Clementine Deliss. Above all, we thank the artists themselves and the lenders to this exhibition (whose names are given separately on page 143) who have been involved through the course of the exhibition and without whom it could not have been formed.

Carol Brown
Barbican Art Gallery

John Picton

TECHNOLOGY, TRADITION AND LUREX:
THE ART OF TEXTILES IN AFRICA

In 1969 Salami Ogumahi came to see me. I was in Okene, his home town and administrative centre of the Ebira-speaking people, in Nigeria. *Ogumahi* was the informal title given to the specialists in a particular species of drumming. The drum was made of a medium-sized water-storage pot, and it was the essential basis of any ensemble of musicians at masquerade events. At the night feast of Ekuechi, when the deceased return to enjoy living hospitality, Salami played for Okevere, a singer whose praises included the title *ogugu-ireba*, the Shaker-of-the-Stones-at-the-Entry-to-the-Domain-of-the-Dead. Salami was well known as the leading performer on the leading drum. He was also an adept healer; and he liked cats. He would often call in if passing my house looking for healing plants. This time, in 1969, he told me he wanted a banner; and he wanted me to design it for him.

Some masked performers had started using banners, supporters carrying them in the processions that accompanied their progress through the community. In Ihima district, for example, Ichakoro, a masked performer at the daytime feast of Echane, had two. On one, a soldier was shooting someone (these events were during the civil war in Nigeria), and the picture was captioned 'I trust in God my only medicine' thereby suggesting an energy that was not to be defeated by the magical medicines of one's rivals.

Ichakoro, the masked performer
Ihima district, Ebira, Nigeria, April 1969

Ichakoro's cloak is a factory-printed imitation of cloth woven by Ewe weavers in Ghana for export to the Niger Delta.

The other banner, painted in yellow on maroon by Ariye Signs, proclaimed:

> Greetings are due to all,
> from Ichakoro.
> It is time to display his art.
> Come one! Come all!!

Salami wanted to be in on the latest fashion (he would have been the first *ogumahi* to have a banner) and thereby advertise and assert his place as more than just an accompanist, even to so great a singer. It would remind Okevere just who was drumming for him, and other *ogumahi* who was the best of them. Salami wanted a banner, and he wanted me to design it for him. At his next visit, knowing that most of his audience would read English better than they could Ebira (the transcription of which had yet to be agreed), I proposed:

Salami Ogumahi No.1

It was just what he wanted, so I drew it out for him, and off he went to find someone to make it for him. I did not see him again and have no idea if his banner was sewn according to my design. Moreover, I was more-or-less oblivious to the relatively far-reaching significance of what had happened. For the story reiterates the efficacy of a simple clear message, particularly in circumstances of an emergent literacy. That, at least, is obvious; but it is also about local agency. For he was the patron and I was the client, he the master, I the servant, albeit one with skills he needed but did not have, enabling me to serve his patronage. His request can be placed within a context of developments in education, literacy and advertisement in West Africa over a hundred years or more, yet the agency was his; and the medium was cloth.

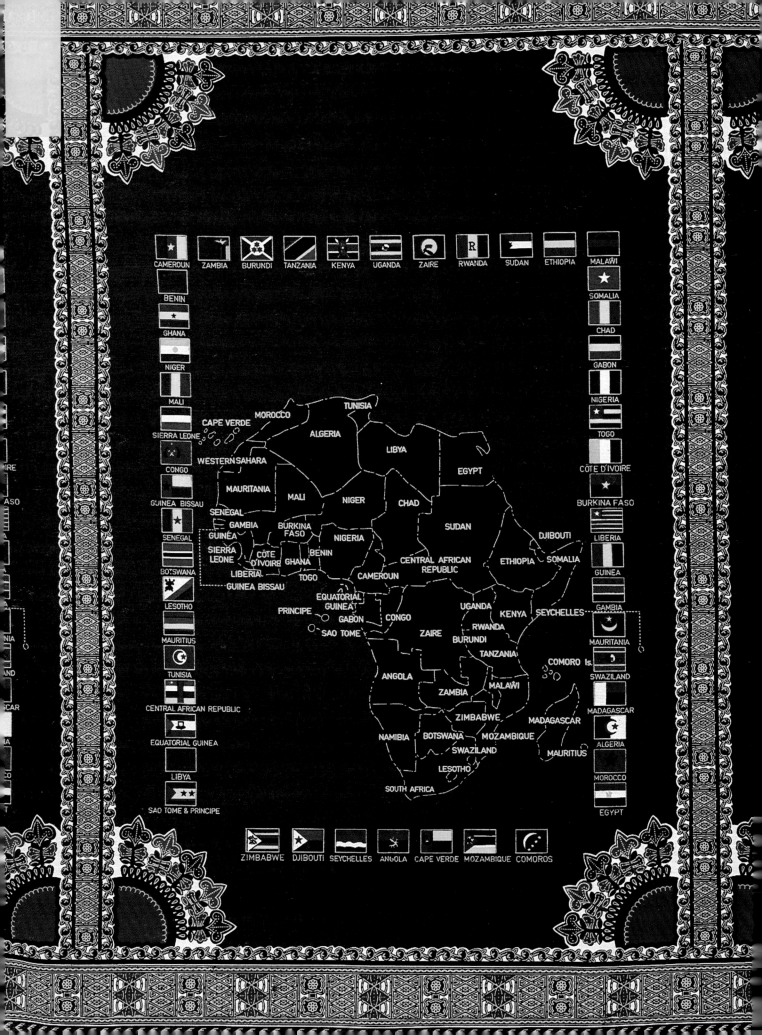

👆 Ten years after I proposed the design for Salami's banner, John Mack and I wrote a book, *African Textiles*, based on material in the British Museum.[1] It accompanied an exhibition, which was later to travel to New York and to Japan, each time expanded to incorporate newly acquired and sometimes newly discovered material.[2] In 1979, there was a small but authoritative literature, based upon first-hand research;[3] and in general it dwelt upon the traditions inherited from the past and on achievements within a given and largely restraining technology, with the developments of the present century considered only in regard to the use of new yarns and other materials within the technology. *African Textiles* followed in that tradition of writing.[4]

👆 In 1989 (another ten years), a second edition of *African Textiles* was published. John Mack wrote a new chapter on Madagascar and, among the large number of rephrasings and corrections, I removed the word 'traditional'. At best it was redundant: it served no useful purpose and signified nothing that was not already obvious. At worst, it was misleading, supposing an essentially 'authentic' African practice. One could write with ease and justification about a textile tradition, in the sense of practice handed on, thus configuring the narrative within temporal and social contexts that imply process and entail at least the possibilities of development. (The idea of context is a particularly apt metaphor of the social environment, deriving of course from the Latin *texere*, to weave.) In contrast, the phrase 'traditional textiles' denotes a category of practice justified by past precedent and essentially unchanging, in contrast to the possibilities of innovation and development. Traditionality was, indeed, exposed as a fiction denoting an invented and perhaps largely spurious authenticity. It was no longer acceptable as a representation of social practice to contrast the 'traditional' with the 'contemporary'. The reality is that traditions entail histories, whereas traditionality closes off the recognition thereof; and that in art as in politics, religion, and so forth, all manner of traditions are contemporary with each other, coexisting, often mutually reflexive, each with its particular temporal status and functional locus.

👆 In any event, while it is impossible to consider life and art in Africa in the absence of textiles, we do not have to presume or invent pan-African continuities as if there were a single narrative account waiting to be written. Even within a single locality, the histories are predictably diverse. For example, Yoruba hand-woven and indigo-dyed textiles can each be construed within a narrative of an emerging ethnic identity, and each is what it is because of the availability of novel materials. Yet in terms of visual impact, technology, and the social, functional or regional locations of production, there is no continuity between these forms of textiles beyond, perhaps, the use of indigo as a dye-

colour or the shape of a Qur'an writing board as a decorative motif. Questions of ethnic, gender and national identities do, of course, figure substantially in the developments of which textiles are a part, and yet there is the danger that we turn an extremely complex set of histories into a mere cliché. However, the

Cotton textile with viscose float-weave Qur'an board motifs
Woven on upright broadloom in imitation of Yoruba *aso oke*
by Ebira women, Nigeria, 1967

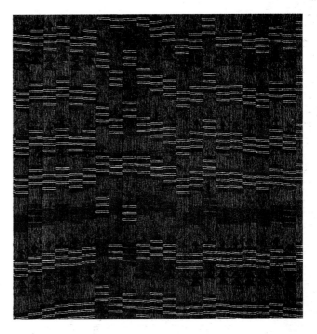

Narrow-strip textile, aso oke, Yoruba, Nigeria, 1960s
Machine-spun cotton with
viscose supplementary float-weave Qur'an board motifs
Collection Judith Appio

Factory-printed cotton
Produced by Whitex, Malawi, c.1993
Private collection

engagement with the aesthetic possibilities of novel yarns, colours and textures, as part of a context (a 'weaving together'), that also includes what we know of developing and emerging identities in the nineteenth and twentieth centuries, can provide us with the very details that enable us to move, usefully, beyond the cliché.

❧ The present exhibition is thus not concerned with the decline and fall of once pristine traditions, nor even with their persistence as such, but rather with the particular range of African responses to and demands upon textiles as a medium of art, especially in the present century. It is about people leading successful lives making and using art, about production and patronage, about constantly revised design agendas thereby maintaining a contemporary relevance. It is about an ability to thrive in competition with all manner of rivals in an Africa that is not all about civil war, corrupt politicians, starving people and infectious diseases. It is about a series of engagements of artists and patrons with materials often, at first, imported from Europe (but now manufactured in Africa); and India (and Indonesia) figure in the narrative also. Although in the late nineteenth century these engagements are largely inscribed within the European scramble for Africa, it is a narrative that subverts and overturns European pretence.

❧ In any case, nineteenth-century engagements between Africa and Europe were hardly novel phenomena, whether via coastal or trans-Saharan trade; and it had always been an engagement shaped and determined by local, African, agency. The exhibition is sometimes about an eclectic response to novelty, but the response is nevertheless an African response determined by local concerns; and more often than we yet realise, when these responses are made within a time of European dominion, in the apparent safety of art that dominion is contested. The inheritance of tradition is, of course, of manifest importance to the present exercise, but the context is the manner in which novel yarns, colours, fabrics and textures have been used in the development of a tradition, not as a mere coda to what has gone before but as of the essence of tradition in Africa.

❧ The emphasis is upon innovative responses to changing circumstances, in which artists have developed traditions of practice by means of the possibilities offered by new materials (yarns, colours, fabrics, textures), images (eg castles, alphabets, the imagery of Islam), technologies (eg the zinc linings of colonial tea chests, sewing machines, roller printers and rotary screens) and demands (eg the contesting of colonial rule, new élite cultures). The intention is thereby to place the traditions inherited from the past within that wider context of the developments of the present century. Sometimes, a particular development may seem minimal: the occasional pink cotton stitching in a piece of Kuba cut-pile embroidery (p.59); the use of European cloth for a Sundi-Kongo fabric coffin (p.57); the use of factory-made cloth in the appliqué festive hangings of Salah El-Din M. El-Ozy in Cairo (and we do not forget that North Africa is Africa too) (p.61). Sometimes, of course, we simply cannot fail to notice: the use of lurex in many parts of West Africa, often in response to a deeply embedded (and, in some places, apotropaic) aesthetic of shininess; the large-scale figurative imagery that has crept into the repertoire of at least one weaver, Oumar Bocoum, in Mali. (p.65)

❧ It would, of course, be easy to suggest that a significant concern of the exhibition is to contrast developments within the traditions inherited from the past with the inception of new traditions.[5] Yet, development within a tradition is sometimes so dramatic as to render the difference that one might wish to sustain in words between the old and the new effectively irrelevant: South African skirts, aprons and so forth, using cloth or vinyl instead of fine rawhide and embellished with glass beads and/or safety pins (p.110);[6] the Hausa gown with sewing-machine embroidery on factory-woven damask (p.76); the Malian habit of cutting factory-made cloth into strips and sewing strips of contrasting colours together as if to replicate the narrow-strip format; the commemorative float-weave pictures in Guinea-Bissau and elsewhere (p.66); the developments in Senegalese weaving initiated by Aissa Dione to produce a broader width of high-fashion cloth; the adaptations of *uli*, the Igbo body-painting tradition, in resist-dyed or hand-painted textiles by Nwakego Okadigwe-Okeke, Ada Udechukwu; or the resist-dyed textiles of Yoruba artists such as Nike Davies, Toyin Oguntona and others.

❧ Sometimes a novel development seems so 'traditional' that we fail to see its novelty and instead take it for granted: the Asante use of silk (p.97) and the Ewe use of machine-spun cotton (p.101);

Afranie Buobu, Bonwire, Asante, hand-stitching strips woven of cotton and rayon/viscose of the design 'Fathia Nkrumah', commemorating Kwame Nkrumah's Egyptian wife, 26 June 1995. The use of rayon/viscose succeeds the silk which Asante weavers are known to have been using since the eighteenth century. In the years leading to Independence, Nkrumah popularised locally woven cloth as signifying national identity.

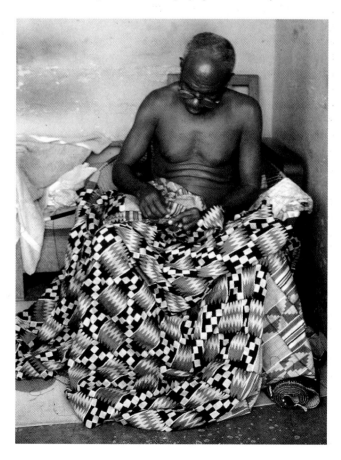

the application of glass beads to a Yoruba king's crown (p.77); the mid-nineteenth-century migration of Mandinka people from Guinea to Sierra Leone and Ivory Coast bringing with them the tie-dyeing and starch- and wax-resist techniques now so characteristic of Sierra Leone (p.69);[7] the Yoruba starch-resist, indigo-dyed cloths made with stencils cut from zinc tea-chest linings (p.16) (and, in the 1960s replicated in silk-screen printing); the application of additional patches to a Kuba appliqué raffia elaborating its appearance with the passage of time (p.59); the development of appliqué design out of the need to patch the holes in a piece of cloth, Kuba again, or the tunics of the followers of Muhammad al Mahdi in the Sudan; the use of factory-made cloth in Anang commemorative *Ngwomo* shrines of south-east Nigeria (p.93);[8] the printed textiles produced in East Africa with a basis in hand-block printing brought to the Swahili coast from India (pp.108-9); and even factory-printed *bogolan* from Mali. Conversely, because a textile is imported from elsewhere we can fail to see it as 'traditional', even when its import is long-standing and the cloth well integrated into local circumstances, for example the cloths imported to the Niger Delta from India and England and the Kalabari habit of cutting and drawing threads out of the cloth to create additional patterning.[9]

🕸 Sometimes, however, the novelty of a particular development within its immediate circumstances seems obvious. Fante war-company flags sewn of imported fabrics according to the pattern of the naval ensign (although even here the imagery responds entirely to local interests in the visual representation of proverbs) (pp.104-5); the Senegalese tapestries woven according to the aesthetic of Negritude as proclaimed by President Senghor (p.34) (yet neither the looms, nor the yarns nor the design processes had any precedent in local practice); the work of the Malian group Bogolan Kasobane and others adapting the *bogolan* method to produce figurative paintings though still using hand-spun cotton cloth;[10] the use of candlewax to resist-dye cloths in 1960s Nigeria (of Sierra Leonean derivation); silk-screen printed textiles by Khamis Chehata of Cairo. The exhibition is also concerned with the development of workshops in many parts of the continent: the tapestries of the Wissa Wassef Art Centre in Egypt, the developments in embroidery, appliqué and tapestry instituted by European enablers in the workshops of southern Africa. Then there are the turn-of-the-century developments of traditions of textile design and manufacture in Europe and in India in response to taste and patronage in Africa: Ebenezer Brown Flemming of Glasgow, the Haarlem Cotton Company, the Manchester-based Calico Printers Association, and their present-day successors including textile design studios and factories in almost every African country.

🕸 It will be obvious that any tradition of art entails a particular technology, and a knowledge of its procedures is essential for the full understanding of an artist's work. However, technical matters are not in general explained here as they have already been dealt with elsewhere.[11] Rather, wherever possible, the focus is upon the artist responsible for a given textile or element of form. For even in those historical or ethnographic contexts wherein the identity of the artist is no longer known (for example the Yoruba women painters of starch-resist, indigo-dyed cloth who often mark their

Factory-printed cotton cloth imitating Malian *bogolan*, on sale in the 'African' street market, 116th Street, Haarlem, New York City April 1995

work with an emblematic signature), that identity is palpable in the explorations of form that constitute the textiles themselves. While it is taken for granted that art is a form of social practice, it must be recognised that so much of the literature on African art has been constituted in terms that leave out the voices of the artists, patrons, critics and teachers. One recognises, of course, that there are artists and there are Artists. There are those who produce cloth and there are those whose uses of cloth are overtly ironic, conceptual, parodic, or who make of it a documentary medium. The convention in Europe is to call the first kind of artist a 'craftsperson', but, as the work in this exhibition demonstrates, the making of a piece of cloth is never just the making of a piece of cloth: all textile design is shot through with commentary, irony, concept and parody (admittedly in varying proportions and not necessarily all of the time). In that case it is impossible to sustain the art/craft distinction on the basis of the work itself. Moreover, whatever their overt intentions might have been, the effect of naming the artists responsible for particular cloths, wherever one can, and of including as wide a range of uses of cloth as the space in the gallery will allow, is to problematise the Romantic idea of the Artist[12] even while enabling individual identity to be made apparent.

🕸 A textile is a context of ideas-and-practices that is both prior to and not necessarily dependent upon subsequent usage (the use of a cloth as dress is often in conflict with its design as laid out by the artist). It is for this reason that although dress and fashion are topics that many would think should take precedence they were not selected as the dominant focus of the exhibition. Indeed, they are matters of such complexity that they must await another time. Nevertheless they are never far away, and we do at least take note of the use of cloth in sculpture and in masking, for example, the costumes made by Lawrence Ajanaku that commemorate deceased mothers in the northern Edo community of Okpella in Nigeria (p.95),[13] and the Yoruba ancestral *egungun* costume (below). The subject-matter of the exhibition is diverse, and the textiles selected for display show this more effectively than any words written about them. It was always understood that it would be impossible to provide anything like a definitive or systematic account of all the developments of the past hundred years or so. Nevertheless, I had thought one might provide a comprehensive list so that at least something of each kind of development would be represented. In the event, even that hope has been put aside, for it has seemed as if, with every day that passes, some new episode emerges in a series of stories that cannot yet be told within the format of a single exhibition and its catalogue. Perhaps the best we can hope for is that it will provide encouragement for new areas of research to add to the excellent recent work already in hand.

Egungun costume, Ogbomoso, 20th century
Cloth, fibre, and wood with thirteen Roman Catholic Madonna medals
150 cm high
Collection Eric D. Robertson

NIGERIA: ASO OKE, RESIST-DYEING, AND WEAVING BY WOMEN

It is, by now, recognised in the study of African art that the manner in which people manifest a sense of tradition and enable its intervention is by no means a force for stasis; and, as already noted, diverse traditions of practice, whatever their individual temporal status, are literally contemporary with one another. One can stand in a Lagos market and see hand-woven textiles in one direction, factory-printed cloth in another, with skyscrapers beyond the market stalls and (from time to time) masked performers running about. Traditions do not survive by being 'traditional' and the textiles for sale in somewhere such as Jankara market, Lagos, or the markets of Niamey and Bamako, or Agbozume in south-eastern Ghana exhibit continuing experimentation. To European eyes the contemporary use of colour and texture in Yoruba *aso oke* (*aso*, cloth; *oke*, hill, the top of something; *ie* high-status cloth), may seem uncomfortably uninhibited as clothing for men and women, especially with the popularity of lurex since the late 1970s (and the popularity around 1990 of rhinestone appliqué on lurex) which will certainly offend an 'arts and crafts' aesthetic. It is quite literally flashy, and yet it is an aesthetic within many West African traditions that has only come to be fully realised with the advent of the new fibres and colours.

Yoruba is a word that identifies a language spoken by millions of people; and it also identifies a history, an inheritance of tradition and social practice, and a contemporary sense of cultural identity. Since the 1850s Yoruba intellectuals have consistently taken the lead in initiating and defining the study of that language, history and inheritance. Yoruba people were also among the leaders of opposition to colonial rule from the very first in late nineteenth-century Lagos; for they included the descendants of freed slaves returning from Sierra Leone amongst whom there were those educated in a manner that placed them as equals to the white colonial élite. Some of them rejected the English names acquired in Sierra Leone along with the stiff collar, jacket and waistcoat, taking to the wide-sleeved gown, thereby initiating its status as a form of what would become Nigerian national dress.[14] This advertisement of particular dress forms in the formation of modern senses of Yoruba and national identity clearly had far-reaching effects, in the development of textiles that are prestigious, relatively costly, yet thriving in competition with cloth of all kinds and prices, and in the current liveliness of Yoruba textile design.

At the turn of the century, Yoruba weavers had access to locally spun and dyed cotton (making use of indigo) and wild silk, magenta silk obtained from the trans-Saharan trade, and machine-spun ready-dyed cotton from European trade. The range of colours was largely restricted to white, grey, beige, blue, indigo and purple/maroon, with the occasional dash of green, and these remain the dominant colours even though all colours of the rainbow are now available. European silk and rayon initially had little impact, and turn-of-the-century elaboration of dress rather made use of multicoloured damask and satin.[15] Today, hand-spun cotton has effectively disappeared, although local wild silk would still be available; and weavers use machine-spun cotton, viscose (replacing silk/rayon in the period since 1945) and lurex, the shiny plastic Japanese fibres that became available in the 1970s, and the popularity of which is as yet undiminished.

🕯 *Aso oke* is woven on a horizontally mounted double-heddle loom in an extremely long four-inch-wide strip which is cut and sewn together edge to edge to form the cloth as needed for the *agbada*, the man's wide-sleeved gown, or a woman's wrap-around skirt. The basic weave structure remains a predominant warp, with yarn laid in differing colours if stripes are required. The major centres of this tradition are Ilorin, Iseyin and Oyo, indicating that it was very much an art of the central Yoruba-speaking region;[16] and from these centres, cloth continues to be distributed via the major cloth markets of the Yoruba-speaking region and beyond.

🕯 In the course of weaving, the cloth is often embellished with a woven openwork and/or with supplementary-weft float-weave motifs (the latter effected in such manner as to suggest a technical borrowing from the upright broadloom once common amongst Yoruba women : float, here, refers to the way the yarn is not woven in with the weft in a straightforward over-and-under sequence, but in effect 'floats' across two or more warps). Brightly coloured 'silk' (*ie* rayon) seems to have been available in Ilorin from around 1933, but used only in the float-weave embellishments.[17] Over the past thirty years, just as the array of colours and textures has been added to, so too the woven embellishments have become increasingly elaborated. In the 1970s, in particular, there was a dramatic development of an openwork technique, sometimes said to have been an attempt to capitalise on the ban on the import of lace into Nigeria in the stringent years of recovery from the civil war. Now, the latest reports from Pat Oyelola (see pp.41-2) indicate experiment with a broader 5½ inch width : as her recent diary of visits to Yoruba markets suggests, this is an art characterised by rapid swings of fashion within a slowly increasing range of options.

🕯 It used to be said that the double-heddle loom was exclusive to male weavers, but in the Yoruba-speaking region this is no longer the case. Over the past ten years it has become commonplace, in Ibadan and other central Yoruba weaving centres, to see young women in weaving households at the loom. Moreover, in the Ekiti districts of eastern Yoruba, young women are taking to weaving as an occupation, using the double-heddle loom of central Yoruba rather than the less efficient and now largely discarded upright single-heddle loom their mothers would have used. They are weaving aso *oke* and training other young women likewise.[18] Yoruba women are also active in disseminating this technology beyond the Yoruba-speaking region to areas where it was not previously found.[19] Meanwhile, in America the Adewumi family of Ile-Oluji, Ondo, and Brooklyn, New York, proprietors of Nigerian Fabrics and Fashions, are catering for the needs of Nigerians and African-Americans (above right).[20]

🕯 There are two other areas of textile production in which women have been directly involved : indigo-dyeing to produce textiles

Yoruba *agbada* (wide-sleeved gown), and other clothing
Tailored in lurex by Nigerian Fabrics and Fashions
Ile-Oluji, Ondo State, Nigeria, and Brooklyn, New York

known generically as *adire* (together with the more recent development of *kampala*), and the upright single-heddle broadloom referred to above.

🕯 Until the present century indigo was used for dyeing cotton yarn for weaving, and textiles (especially women's wrap-around skirts) for renewed use; and these usages continue. In such contexts the indigo could be resisted, in yarn by tieing before dyeing to produce the effects known as *ikat*, and in cloth by using raffia to stitch or tie sticks and stones to produce relatively large-scale patterns; and this is the background to Yoruba *adire* cloth.[21] Then, with the availability of factory-woven shirting (at first imported but now produced in West Africa), these techniques were transferred to what in effect was a rather different medium. The thinner quality and more even structure of this cloth, when compared with Yoruba hand-spun cotton, enabled the development of a much finer stitching and tieing, though still using raffia. In addition, tailors began stitching cloth by sewing machine; and dyers in Abeokuta and Ibadan (both cities in Nigeria

¶ *Oloba* (lit. 'that with a king'), indigo-dyed cotton cloth, starch-resist applied by stencil, probably from Abeokuta, and almost certainly prepared in celebration of the Silver Jubilee of King George V and Queen Mary, 1935
Collection George Jackson

☛ Stencil used in the preparation of *adire*, cut from tinned sheet-iron, Abeokuta, Yoruba, Nigeria. The 'Abiola Babes' are a local football team, sponsored by Alhaji M.K.O. Abiola (winner of the aborted 1993 election).

¶ *Oloba*, design prepared for the 1935 Jubilee reworked for the coronation of Edward VIII, 1936
Collection Helen Travers

that originated in the mid-nineteenth-century refugee camps to which people were dispersed by the wars of the period) developed the use of starch as a resist agent. At Abeokuta stencils were cut from the zinc linings of missionary and colonial tea-chests (themselves bearing stencilled instructions), while at Ibadan the designs that emerged were copied by the freehand painting of starch onto the cloth before dyeing.[22]

🌑 *Adire* is the 'classic' example of a 'traditional' textile that is nothing of the kind: rather, it is a form that effectively takes apart the very notion of traditionality. This medium has facilitated an expansion of the repertoire of form and subject matter, and thereby the scope of the concerns that could be addressed, beyond all likeness with the past. This repertoire: the pillars of Ibadan town hall, King George V with Queen Mary, and the horse of the Holy Prophet of Islam, has been explored elsewhere.[23] Less well known, however, is the transfer of the design from the British Royal Jubilee of 1935 (top) to the coronation of King Edward VIII (right). The stencil cutters of Abeokuta were ahead of the expected demand only to find themselves frustrated when the coronation did not happen. The design was not recut for King George VI.

In the 1960s, from the markets of Lagos to the villages of north-eastern Ekiti, one could see extant all the phases of this development, although since then the production of *adire* has slowly declined though not quite disappeared. The reasons for this are not altogether clear, but must include its development from a domestic tradition of no particular esteem; the ready availability of factory-printed cloth; the education of women; and the development of *kampala* (a fashion named after the Kampala Peace conference during the Nigerian civil war where the design is formed as women sprinkle molten candlewax rather wildly over the cloth).

Ibadan and Abeokuta were not the only centres for the production of *adire*, of course: Nike Olaniyi-Davies relates how as a young woman brought up in the village of Ogidi, in the Ijumu area beyond Ekiti, she would visit Oshogbo where her mother's sister made *adire* cloth.[24] In due course, Nike herself was to settle in Oshogbo and began embroidering costumes for the members of Twins Seven-Seven's band; and in order to speed up the process she, too, took to producing hand-painted and stencilled starch-resist cloths. Then, Nike tells us, 'during the Nigerian civil war people began to make this *kampala*. There was a woman near our house doing it and I said to her: "I want to learn how to do this".' While the precise details are not available, Toyin Oguntona reports that in response to the prohibition on the importing of factory-printed textiles during the 1967-9 civil war, 'various backyard dyeing industries sprang up . . . petty traders, labourers, farmers, clerks and the jobless suddenly became overnight *kampala* dyers. . .'[25]

Kampala was indeed one of the more evident developments in local textile production in Nigeria in the late 1960s, using factory dyes either in simple folded and tied resist-dyed patterns, or with the spattered effect achieved with the use of hot wax as the resist agent. Subsequently, a block printing technique was developed for applying the wax to the cloth, and this has now substantially supplanted the *adire* tradition as a means of producing relatively cheap decorative textiles. Meanwhile, Nike Olaniyi-Davies integrated the distinctive qualities and techniques of *adire* and *kampala* in the use of the very finely detailed wax-resist indigo-dyed fabric pictures for which she is so well known, to become perhaps the most successful (certainly the most subtle) exponent of the Oshogbo phantastic;[26] and for the past ten years she has had her studio and gallery in Oshogbo, whilst exhibiting and running workshops also in Britain and America.

Resist-dyeing has also entered the curriculum of the Fine Art departments of Nigerian universities. Dr Toyin Oguntona, a senior lecturer at Ahmadu Bello University, Zaria, for example, practises and teaches within the Faculty of Environmental Design, using tied and starch-resist techniques as well as screen and wax printing (p.71). Although born near Lagos, his education took him out of the Yoruba-speaking area to Minna and Benin City in Nigeria, to Kumasi, Ghana (BA), Pakistan (Diploma in Textile Technology), and Madison, Wisconsin (MA, PhD). These life-histories develop the theme already established of the creative openness of Africa, in which new fibres, materials, textures and techniques are used to address local concerns. Oguntona's international training is characteristic of many present-day artists

and it illustrates the impossibility of linking the artist to any particular status or identity. The comparison with Nike Olaniyi-Davies reinforces this, for despite the obvious differences of access to formal training and education, each is working with textiles in a manner that is related to *adire*, and each is part of an international network as a result. Moreover, just as the weaving of *aso oke* has moved beyond 'traditional' boundaries, so has resist-dyeing. For in the work of Nwakego Okadigwe-Okeke and Ada Udechukwu, among others, the Igbo body-painting forms of *uli* have been adapted using these techniques.

A third area of textile history in Nigeria concerns the upright single-heddle broadloom used by women (below). Given that the entire work of this loom is done with the hands, unlike the double-heddle looms in which the feet are used to shed the warp, this loom is a technically less efficient piece of apparatus. Nevertheless it has thrived in many parts of the country, and only now is its use being edged out as young women turn to the horizontal double-heddle loom.[27] In Nigeria, this loom was to be found widely distributed through the Yoruba-, Edo- and Igbo-speaking peoples and by the beginning of this century it had spread to the peoples of the Benue and Middle Niger regions. Throughout, it was among the domestic arts of women, and its survival was inevitably jeopardised by the advent of relatively cheap factory-printed cotton cloth. At Independence in 1960 its use survived only in rural areas or as a result of very particular developments in design responding to local fashion demands in much the same way as *aso oke*. In the Yoruba-speaking region this loom was obsolescent, production having been largely supplanted by *adire*, *aso oke*, and factory-printed and/or woven cloth.

Agnes Omaku,
with the loom she had set up
with supplementary shed sticks to facilitate
float-weave patterns
Karaworo, Okene, Ebira, Nigeria, 1968

Senior members of Osugbo association at Ijebu-Igbo, Yoruba, Nigeria, 1969.
The two men seated front left are wearing *aso olona* woven at Ijebu-Ode.
The man standing back right is wearing cloth also patterned with weft floats
and probably woven in Ilorin.

In contrast, in the more remote north-easterly communities of Ekiti and Kabba, together with northern Edo, Ebira and Igbo peoples, women continued to weave both domestic and high-status fabrics, still using hand-spun cotton, giving the impression of a single tradition with local variants, but also using machine-spun and viscose yarns in a variety of local decorative forms. Much of this production was for local use, though the villages of Okene and Akwete (Ebira and southern Igbo respectively) had developed reputations throughout Nigeria for decorative weaving with the result that textiles from these locations had wide circulation in the country. At Okene this development was brought about by a local chief who appears to have facilitated access to the weft-float technique and to rayon yarn through his contacts with the Yoruba-speaking city of Ilorin. By the 1960s, Ebira women were experimenting with a design repertoire that drew upon diverse sources, including *aso oke* and the patterns characteristic of Akwete (see opposite). Moreover, this kind of weaving had spread to Nupe and Hausa peoples possibly from an Oyo-Yoruba source.

Another place where this loom is used is the southern Yoruba city of Ijebu-Ode.[28] Here, patterned textiles (*aso olona*) are characterised by supplementary float-weave motifs representing water animals, such as crocodiles and mudfish, with local connotations of authority via emblematic association with Olokun, god of the sea and of wealth. As it happens, almost the entire set of motifs can be derived from a single basic set of geometric forms, so perhaps it is not surprising that when these textiles were transported across the Niger Delta and, in due course, replicated by weavers in the southern Igbo community of Akwete, the details of emblematic representation were lost. For the crocodile is reinterpreted as a tortoise, and these cloths become known generically as 'Tortoise cloth'.

The question is: just how did this transfer of motifs come about? While the answer is not altogether certain, we do know that trade in textiles from southern Yoruba and Edo eastwards to the Niger Delta was reported as institutionalised in the early sixteenth century. In the eastern Niger Delta, the distinctive cloths from Ijebu came to be essential within ritual and ceremonial contexts, and these textiles are still extant in the cloth treasuries of the area. Then, when the supply was disturbed from the 1850s onwards by the pressures exerted by European traders, one can imagine Kalabari and/or other Delta inhabitants going to Akwete as the nearest location of weavers known to them, to encourage

Cotton cloth with rayon thread, Akwete, Igbo, Nigeria
Collected in the late 1930s by G.I.Jones
178 cm long
Collection Fowler Museum of Cultural History
University of California
Los Angeles (MCH X84-3)

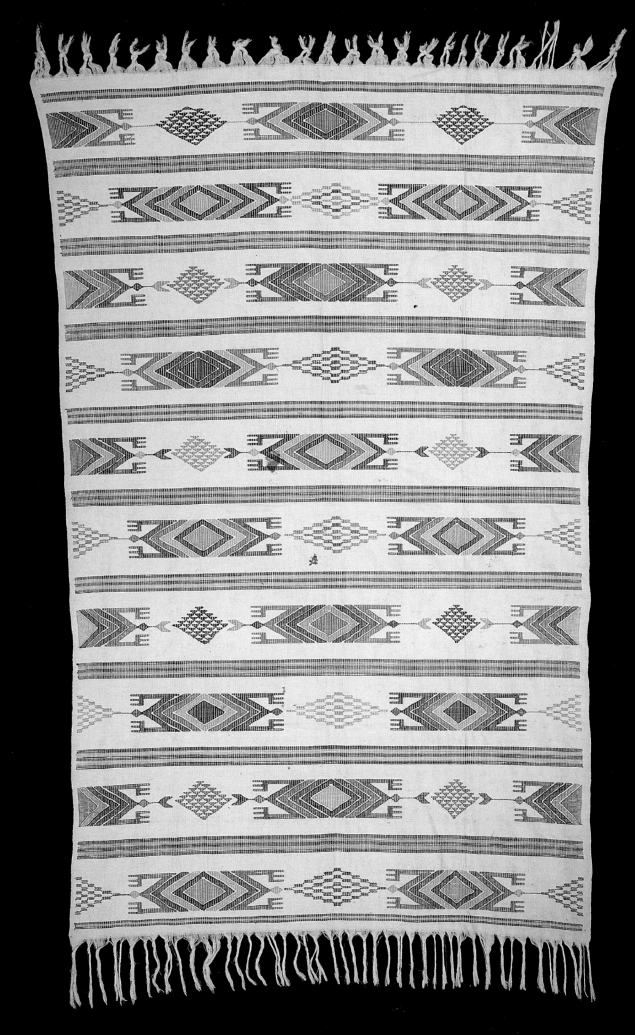

them to reinvent the necessary technical means with which to reproduce the Ijebu designs. Certainly, no Akwete cloth is known that has been woven from anything other than factory-made ready-dyed yarn, yarns which, indeed, would have been available to the Delta traders through their contacts with Europeans. In the present century, Akwete women realised the market potential of their work and began to sell it in Lagos and elsewhere. In consequence, although beyond the Ijebu kingdoms no one had heard of Ijebu-Ode as a centre for decorative weaving, by the 1960s Akwete had an established Nigeria-wide reputation for fine weaving, so much so that women elsewhere (including Ebira) were imitating the designs.

Textiles have also long been imported into the Niger Delta from Keta, a coastal Ewe-speaking location in south-east Ghana. They are easily identifiable by the characteristic alternation of warp-faced and weft-faced striping in a four-inch wide strip of cloth. In the Delta this type of cloth is known as *popo* after the coastal trading ports of Grand and Little Popo in what is now Togo. In the 1930s an unknown Ewe weaver had come from Keta to the southern Igbo town of Aba and set up his loom. Then, in 1937 Christopher Brown from the Ibani region of the eastern Delta had apprenticed himself to Ewe weavers in Keta and upon his return began to train young men and women as his own apprentices. Delta weavers, while retaining the characteristic format as described, have simplified the design to stark contrasts between the warp- and weft-faced areas. Meanwhile, Akwete women began to imitate these distinctive patterns on the broadloom (with far greater ease, it should be stressed, than European attempts to replicate Asante and Ewe design).

Although some measure of trans-Saharan trade is probably as old as the Sahara, documentary evidence is only available in the writings of Islamic writers from the eighth century AD onwards;[29] and we know that textiles certainly figured in this trade, in both directions. There is also some evidence (implied within aspects of weave structure and textile design) for sub-Saharan attempts to compete with cloths imported from North Africa. The logic of the narrow-strip format is such that it enables the bold juxtapositioning of pattern in the edge-to-edge sewing together of individual strips. This is most obvious when there is a weft-faced structure enabling a weft-wise patterning. Yet, there are cloths woven very deliberately to align a weft-wise design across the entire face of the cloth thereby apparently denying that logic. Perhaps this was a response to the broadloom tapestry-weave cloths woven by Berber women for export southwards. The well-known *khasa*, woollen blankets woven by the Maboube weavers of the inland delta region of the River Niger in Mali are a case in point; and these may well have been traded northwards[30] as well as all over West Africa. In any case, their essential status within aspects of Asante ceremonial is part of the background to the evolution of forms now distinctive of Asante textiles.[31]

The Asante confederacy is a grouping of Akan kingdoms, recognising the authority of the kingdom of Kumasi, whose king is the Asantehene. Akan is the name given to communities and kingdoms speaking the Twi language in southern Ghana and Ivory Coast. Not all Akan kingdoms are, or ever were, part of the Asante confederacy, which came into being in the late seventeenth century and dominated the trade networks linking savanna and coast in this part of West Africa, in particular

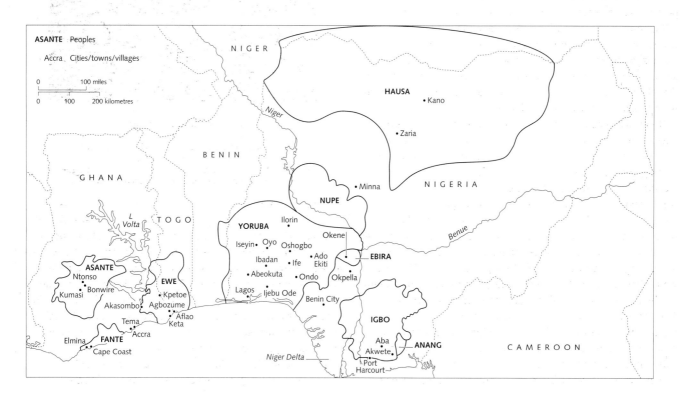

controlling access to the Akan goldfields. Its steadily increasing prestige, influence, wealth and authority through the eighteenth and nineteenth centuries, and restriction on the use of silk to chiefly hierarchies and their courts, provided a context in which weavers appear to have been pressed into formal experiment within the limits of their technical means.[32]

🖌 A good deal of Asante cloth, certainly in the past, was woven of cotton, locally hand-spun to a fine quality unequalled elsewhere, and dyed in indigo to permit a seemingly endless variety of striped patterns. However, by the 1730s Asante weavers were also unravelling silk cloths from Europe to use the yarn in their own textiles. The characteristic features of Asante weaving include the use of silk, the alternation of warp-faced and weft-faced plain weave within a single length of cloth, made possible by means of the addition to the loom of a second pair of heddles, and the use of float-weave motifs over the warp-faced areas as well. Silk may have been used sparingly at first in the weft-faced and float-weave patterning, but in due course, perhaps by the close of the eighteenth century,[33] it became habitual to weave the entire cloth of silk. In the past, silk textiles were only woven on commission from members of the royal and chiefly élite and were only to be found on sale in the market-place if rejected. Cotton has continued to be woven into the present century for general use although the shortage of supplies of the hand-spun yarn from the savanna to the north has meant that Asante weavers made increasing use of imported yarn.[34] By the mid-nineteenth century, Asante weavers were probably using more European machine-spun cotton than they were hand-spun yarn.[35]

🖌 Textiles known as *adwinasa* and *asasia* represent the high points of achievement in the development of technical and formal skill among the weavers of Bonwire, not far from Kumasi, which was the locus of all Asante silk weaving. *Adwinasa* means 'fullness of ornament' (*adwini*, ornament, motif, artifice), and the layout is such that the weft-faced banding has been reduced to the minimum required to provide a formal structure within which the entire face of the cloth could be embellished with float-weave patterns, with each element of design subject to variations of scale, configuration and colour to ensure, in the finest *adwinasa* of the late nineteenth century, the absence of exact repetition.[36] The significances of the individual motifs are various and include items of weaving apparatus, chiefly regalia, proverbial connotations and historical references, although the main emphasis is upon the visual pleasure taken in formal elaboration, within the context of chiefly authority. *Asasia* was the name given to silk cloths woven only to the commission of the Asantehene and distinguished by the use of a third pair of heddles.[37] *Asasia* were laborious to produce, and of the highest status, but did not exhibit the same degree of formal experiment as *adwinasa*.

🖌 Another and very different Asante textile is *adinkra*, in which mostly non-figurative emblems are printed onto an otherwise plain textile using stamps cut from pieces of calabash with a glutinous black pigment. The emblems each have specific proverbial connotations, but they are not used with any kind of

Signboard advertising the sale of textiles
Bonwire, Asante, Ghana, 1993
Painted by Kumasi painter, Nana Elvis (also known as Elvis Presley).

Arrangement of heddles on loom,
Bonwire, Asante, Ghana, November 1993.
The pair to the left groups the warps into units of six; weaving with these produces a weft-faced plainweave. The heddles to the right serve to alternate every other warp element; weaving with these produces a warp-faced plainweave.

syntactic intention, rather as a more general presentation of moral principle. Recently, figurative designs (eg the *sankofa* bird, looking backwards to remind us that we should not be afraid to learn from past mistakes), the Mercedes-Benz logo, and lettering have appeared as *adinkra* stamps. *Adinkra* production is mostly located at Ntonso, near Kumasi, Ghana, which is also a centre for weaving cotton and lurex. The earliest example of these cloths in the British Museum was collected in 1817 and is very similar to present-day examples, except that the cloth, though still woven in narrow strips, is no longer of hand-spun cotton. In any case, much of the *adinkra* produced today is hand printed onto factory-made shirting, though damask, velour, and factory-

Asafo (war-company) flag
Fante, Ghana, early 20th century
Collection Peter Adler

Fante flag dancing
at annual path-clearing festival (Akwambo)
Legu, Ghana
1975

printed cloth are also used. If the cloth used is black, brown, red or purple it is worn for the period from the death to the burial of the deceased person whom one is mourning. Printed on white cloth, the significance is rather one of post-burial celebration. *Adinkra* cloths are now imitated in textiles printed in the Ivory Coast and the Netherlands.

The Akan interest in proverbs is, of course, proverbial, and is manifest in the visual arts particularly in the consideration and exercise of chiefly and royal authority. However, in the field of textiles the political, the proverbial and the visual come together most obviously on Fante flags.

Fante is the southernmost dialect of Twi spoken in a series of small coastal states which, historically, affected a measure of involvement and control in regard to the presence of European traders. This entailed inter- and intra-state rivalry, hence the military companies, *asafo*, for which the flags were made.[38] The very specific relationship between flags, their subject matter and their proverbial connotations cannot be underestimated, given the exercise of authority and the bonds of identity and competition enacted in the existence and practices of *asafo*. Here, in contrast to the benign symbols of *adinkra*, the challenge to one's rivals is proclaimed by the imagery of the flag. (pp.104-5)

The source of *asafo* flag form is clear from the small rectangular inset that echoes that of the flags of European, mostly British, ships, although from 1957 the form of that rectangle is changed from Union Jack to Black Star (p.105). The remainder of the flag provides a field of usually one colour applied to which are pieces of cloth of contrasting colours cut to the shapes, variously, of people, animals, plants, pools of water, atmospheric phenomena, monsters, enemas, aeroplanes and other artifacts; and for the most part, these images are immediately recognisable.

The reasons for their selection and juxtaposition will not be so obvious, however, and will depend upon proverbial connotations appropriate to the circumstances of the making of any given flag. Flags are intended to challenge; but they are also a source of knowledge of proverbs, and a means by which these proverbs exist.

The frontal emphasis characteristic of so much in the figurative art traditions of sub-Saharan Africa is absent. Figures are more often than not shown in profile with the occasional three-quarter view (though very occasionally there is that Cubist visual trick in which the human head is represented from the front and from the side in the one image, as illustrated opposite). People and animals are often evidently in movement, and there is sometimes a slogan of letters and/or numbers that may or may not reiterate the proverbial connotations of the imagery. The textiles used are European, sometimes cut from damask table cloths, though lightweight cotton is more usual.

The sewing of emblematic devices to a rectangular piece of cloth intended for display as an index of identity is widespread. Flags bearing appliqué Islamic texts were to be found across the Sahel regions of Africa with the armies of reform, including the Fulani *jihad*, initiated by Usman dan Fodio in the early nineteenth century, or the late nineteenth-century holy war of Muhammad al Mahdi in what is now the Sudan Republic. In the kingdom of Danhome, appliqué banners advertised the exploits of its kings; and on the coast of West Africa the flags of European traders would have been in evidence from the late fifteenth century. They were among the gifts regularly presented to any chief with whom one wanted to effect and maintain a trading relationship,

and Fante leaders certainly did not have a monopoly on these artifacts. Indeed, among the earliest references to flags by European visitors is to the flag flown in 1693 by the Akwamu general (Akan, but not Fante) who had captured Christiansborg Castle. In this instance, the description of the figure of a man bearing a scimitar suggests a flag made according to local expectation; and we know that flags were commissioned in Europe with the aim of conforming to local taste (the British Museum has one on which a whale is embroidered making its way though a mass of icebergs). Augustus Casely-Hayford found that others were embroidered by Irish nuns. In any case, the evidence of the sheer numbers of Fante flags themselves suggests a proliferation of this form in a developing context of rivalry seemingly for its own sake, that is for social purposes no longer related to the conduct of war, following upon the increasing domination of the area by the British in the course of the nineteenth century. At Cape Coast, for example, as from the 1860s all flags had to be registered with the Governor as a measure of control.

The emblematic requirements of a Fante flag are manifestly different from Islamic and European examples. So too, obviously, are the particular skills of flag dancing, and the other artifacts, especially the *posuban*. These cement monuments were developed in the late nineteenth century to provide a more-or-less permanent visual focus for the *asafo*. Also embellished with emblematic devices, they are used to store the flags and drums of the association.

The forms of the Fante flag provide for the articulation of proverbs in a context of performance in which verbal discourse,

Painted graves near Denu Junction on road to Ho, Ewe, Ghana, March 1994.
Two different styles of Ewe weaving are represented.

mere oratory, would be ineffective. Moreover, the proverbial connotations make possible a declaration, a narrative and a commentary about the rivalry between *asafo* that is distinctively Akan.

The Ewe-speaking peoples live to the east of the Akan in southern Ghana and adjacent Togo. Their local ritual practices display certain continuities eastwards with the peoples of Danhome and western Yoruba. Status and authority in an Ewe community, however, take on an Akan look, and this is manifest in superficial aspects of Ewe weaving. Ewe weavers employ the same kind of loom as Asante weavers, that is with two pairs of heddles (p.21), enabling the alternation of warp-faced and weft-faced patterning within the four-inch-wide format to produce *adanudo*, 'skilled cloth';[39] and, as with Asante textiles, the weaving is planned such that when the strip as woven is cut and sewn together edge to edge, a regular ordering of design is apparent. The precise relationship between these traditions remains to be investigated,[40] and while such evidence as there is suggests a common derivation from the north, the fact that these are the only two traditions in which two pairs of heddles are used also suggests the possibility of 'ethnographic espionage'.

There are in fact many differences between Asante and Ewe weaving. Firstly, Asante weavers at Bonwire developed the use of silk, whereas Ewe weavers have made far greater use of ready-dyed cotton and a wider range of colours. In 1785, weavers at Aflao, Ghana, were seen unravelling European red cotton cloths,[41] a well-saturated red being almost impossible to achieve with West African vegetable and mineral dye colours. Moreover, there are at least four centres of Ewe weaving in south-eastern Ghana and adjacent Togo, each with its particular range of design forms (in contrast to the one centre of Asante silk weavers).

Textiles woven at Kpetoe, Ghana, for example, display warp-faced and weft-faced areas more-or-less equally spaced permitting the regular alternation of blocks of colour (although not the only configuration typical of Kpetoe). One of the styles of weaving in the Agbozume/Keta region is a plain self-coloured 'silk' textile with brightly contrasting figurative float-weave motifs: scorpions, hands, elephants, butterflies, cockerels, stools, swords, divination apparatus, crowns, parrots, a ship's anchor, forks, people and so forth. Ewe weavers indeed employ figurative motifs and also lettering in their float-weave embellishments; and they habitually ply cotton yarn of two colours, at Agbozume/Keta in the warp stripes, at Kpetoe in the weft-faced areas. Asante weavers do none of this. Ewe weavers also often imitate Asante designs in order to make the most of the demand for *kente*, as a form of national dress.

There were, and still are, other differences: the commissioning of highly patterned cloth was not limited to members of an Ewe chiefly élite (although even in Asante this is no longer the case with the emergence of a national dress); and Ewe weavers, in any case, worked more to the market than on commission, with not only a greater variety of styles associated with different weaving centres but also with patterns intended to supply outside demands such as the Kongo cloths woven for the eastwards coastal trade. Perhaps these include the so-called Popo cloth woven for sale in the Niger Delta, as discussed above.

The concluding part of this essay is, in its way, a complex and elaborate counterpart to the vignette drawn from my experience of working in Nigeria with which I began. It is concerned with the cotton textiles produced initially in Europe for sale in West and Central Africa, although now also produced in factories in most African countries; and they are the subject of a small but steadily increasing Africanist literature.[42] The cloths are of two kinds. The so-called wax prints are produced by printing a resin paste onto both faces of the cloth, matching exactly, and treating it mechanically in order to produce the characteristic cracking effects. The cloth is dyed, usually in indigo, which is resisted by the resin paste. After this paste is removed other colours are added, preferably by hand using wooden printing blocks (which makes the cloth more expensive as a result). Successive applications of colour will not match exactly and this allows the cloth to 'sparkle'.[43] They are the more complex to produce and, in consequence, the more expensive; and the differences of cost and quality are recognised throughout West Africa.

Fancy prints, in contrast, are printed on one face only, with designs that draw upon the same repertoire as the wax (that is resin-resist) prints. They were formerly printed by means of engraved metal rollers, though now rotary screens are used (screen-printing screens mounted on rollers). Several techniques were evolved, including particular effects obtained by the discharge of colour, and an extensive terminology that includes green grounds, bleeders, Java prints, super prints, imitation wax, guaranteed imitation wax, roller prints; but none of them makes use of resin.[44]

One might argue, of course, that, as these fabrics are the products of European industry, they have no real place here; and

Page of ledger
Vlisco factory museum, Helmond, Netherlands
The earliest explicit reference to textiles printed specifically for the coast of West Africa
August 1852

this view may well account for their relatively late entry into the subject matter of Africanist art-historical research. Moreover, this opinion might seem to be reinforced by the colonial encouragement of any attempt to subvert local hand-production by the import of cheap alternatives, thereby transferring wealth from Africa to Europe. However, the facts of the history of wax and fancy prints turns this view of things on its head. Two European companies still produce wax prints for sale in Africa: Vlisco (van Vlissingen in Helmond, the Netherlands), and ABC (Arthur Brunnschweiler & Co. at the Newton Bank Printworks, Hyde near Manchester); and it is evident from their various archives, firstly that these developments were contingent upon a local agency with a far greater determining role than has hitherto been realised, and secondly that the employees of these firms are kept in employment by African patronage.[45]

The exercise of that agency and patronage was contingent upon a series of prior factors, including the distribution of indigo throughout West Africa with its particular technologies of production and use. There was also the development of indigo-dyeing in several European countries, typically with little white patterns on a dark ground suitable for women's clothing, scarves and handkerchiefs; and the earliest explicit reference to cloth for West Africa in the books at the museum and archives of Vlisco shows samples of this kind, dated August 1852 (opposite). In any case, the sale of European textiles in West Africa is as old as the European exploration of the coastal route to India (and we have already noted the importance of silk and cotton yarns in Asante and Ewe weaving). Other relevant factors include the African interest in proverbs as a form of discourse about social relationships, the image and idea of the hand as a means of self-empowerment, and the fact that the late nineteenth century was the period in which a literate education emerged in colonial Africa both to serve and to subvert the pretentions of Empire.

In the reconstruction of the Netherlands textile industry in the period after the defeat of Napoleon and the subsequent secession of Belgium (and thus the departure from the Dutch economy of Flemish textile production), textile mills were established in Haarlem, including a 'Turkey Red' dyeworks and the Belgian printers Previnaire & Co, which later amalgamated to form the Haarlem Cotton Company (Haarlemsche Katoen Maatschappij). It was reckoned that it ought to be possible to replicate Indonesian batiks by methods that would be cheaper than the local use of a pen with a small reservoir of molten wax, and to this end J.B.T. Previnaire had adapted a French banknote-printing machine, nicknamed as a result 'la Javanaise', to print a resin-resist on each face of the cloth. However, almost immediately 'la Javanaise' was succeeded by an adapted duplex form of the engraved-roller printing machine previously invented and patented by Thomas Bell, a Scotsman, in 1783. Indian and Netherlands textile producers had also been experimenting with the possibilities of hand-blocking imitation batiks (the origin of the Java print, of which the earliest examples in the Vlisco archives are dated to between 1846-9), and this technique had been introduced to Indonesia in the middle of the century as a means of applying the wax to the fabric before dyeing. Indian textiles, both woven and printed, especially the chintz fabrics hand-blocked with small floral motifs, were already popular in West Africa. Chintz in particular was replicated widely in an English cotton industry that was also aware of the commercial possibilities of Indonesian batik-type production. Hand-block

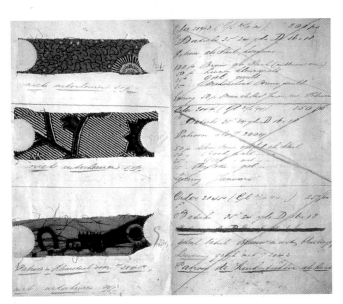

Haarlem Cotton Company order book for 1904-6
Order no.2145 (from Glasgow) dated 25 November 1904
for 'Sword of Kingship' design
Collection Vlisco, Helmond

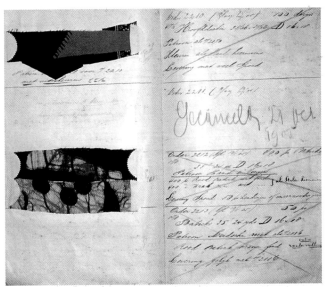

Haarlem Cotton Company order book for 1904-6
Order no.2212 (from Glasgow) dated 31 January 1905
for hands and fingers design
Collection Vlisco, Helmond

printing was also introduced from India to the Swahili coast of East Africa, leading to another and rather different set of developments.

The products of Previnaire's inventions were not particularly successful, as the application of resin paste by means of duplex rollers inadvertently produced cracking and bubbling effects that were not acceptable to Indonesian taste; and it proved difficult to control the application of a second colour. Yet they were found to sell in West Africa. Two further factors must now be introduced. Firstly, when the Dutch ceded their West Africa territories to the British in 1872, many of the mercenary soldiers recruited on the Gold Coast to assist in the establishment of their East Indian colonies returned to settle in places like Elmina, where there had been a Dutch presence, perhaps bringing with them a taste for Indonesian batik.[46] Secondly, there was the agency of Ebenezer Brown Flemming of Glasgow, 1858-1912, born into a family of Flemish (and textile-producing) origin, and first described as a dealer in 'Turkey Red', then as an East India merchant, finally as founder of Brown Flemming Ltd, Dyers and Printers of African and Colonial Specialities. Whether he ever set foot in Africa is unclear, although he was involved with and would have been informed about West Africa as a result of the missionary activities of his Presbyterian church connections on the Gold Coast, and his trading activities, with feedback from the women in the market.

Haarlem Cotton Company *sibi saba* or 'cushion cover' design
Printed by Rossingh Veenedal *c*.1925
Collection A.Brunnschweiler & Co., Hyde

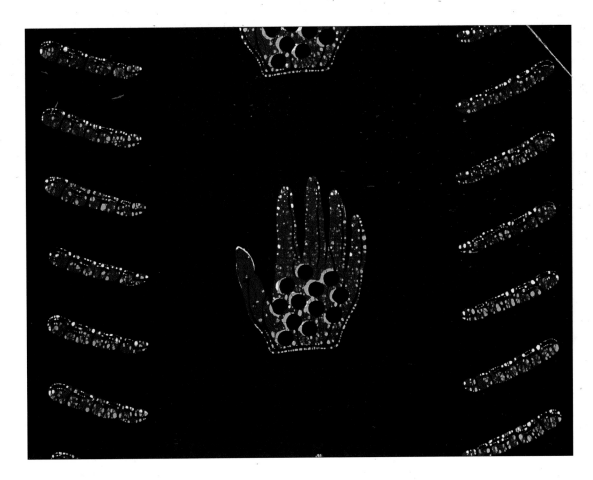

Probable original printing by Haarlem Cotton Company
of 'Hands and Fingers' design, c.1904-5
Collection A.Brunnschweiler & Co., Hyde

Variation of 'Hands and Fingers' design with gold coins
possibly by Haarlem Cotton Company, undated
Collection A.Brunnschweiler & Co., Hyde

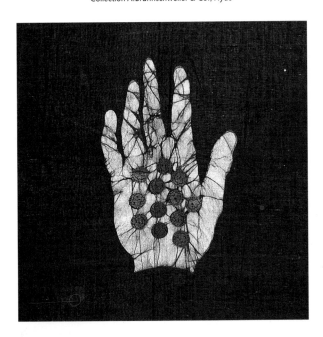

This, then, is the context in which the Haarlem Cotton Company began their flawed attempts to engrave rollers with designs based upon Indonesian batiks, but now specifically intended for the West African market. Ebenezer Brown Flemming of Glasgow was their sole agent, responsible for marketing the cloths and, one imagines (but cannot prove), for feeding back information about their success or otherwise. Unfortunately, no evidence has yet come to light that enables specific events to be dated precisely (even assuming that we knew what the specific events were). Nevertheless, it appears that around 1900 Brown Flemming was registering the Haarlem designs in Britain in his own name. In itself this mattered little as long as the Haarlem Cotton Company was in business, and he was its agent; but in 1912 he died and in 1917 the Haarlem Cotton Company closed. The printing rollers were bought by Vlisco, which took it for granted that in doing so it was buying the copyright of the designs. The Brown Flemming company continued in business until 1939 when it was taken over by Grafton for the Manchester Calico Printers Association, which considered that thereby it had acquired the copyright. Not unsurprisingly, the so-called Brown Flemming designs subsequently became the focus for litigation, also involving Japanese manufacturers, which concluded by

Configuration of ancient Egyptian motifs
known as 'The Mummy'
Early printing by Haarlem Cotton Company
Sent for registration, 1912
Collection A. Brunnschweiler & Co., Hyde

Dutch countryside
Printed by Haarlem Cotton Company
Sent for registration, 1912
Did not go into production
Collection A. Brunnschweiler & Co., Hyde

determining that it was impossible to establish which of them had prior rights to the Brown Flemming designs.

🖎 The earliest documented record of any of this is the *HKM Stalenboek 1 1904-1906* (HKM = Haarlemsche Katoen Maatschappij), which documents orders for particular designs in specific colourways (in addition to indigo) that were coming from Glasgow. The name of Brown Flemming is not there, but the probability has to be that the orders were coming from him. Order no.2145, dated 25 November 1904 (p.25) is for the pattern known variously as 'Corkscrew' and 'Sword of Kingship', a design based upon a wrought iron Asante ceremonial sword in the British Museum (BM Ethno 1896.5-19.4). Accompanied by a small sample, this indicates that that design was in production; and likewise order no.2212, dated 31 January 1905, for the hands and fingers design (p.25); and order no. 2296 of 19 April 1905, for the design based upon postage stamps and the various ports of the colonial Gold Coast. These motifs, though placed within a style derived from Indonesian batik, are clearly themselves derived from a 'Gold Coast' rather than an Indonesian source.

🖎 Indeed, the decorative style, layout and subject matter of the earliest Brown Flemming cloths in the Vlisco and Brunnschweiler archives indicate that whoever was responsible for advising the Haarlem engravers was drawing upon Indonesian and ancient Egyptian visual sources, West African proverbial and educational interests, and the Dutch countryside; and all rendered in a style derived from Indonesian batik.

🖎 The specifically Indonesian designs included 'Night and Day' (with a diagonal separation between light and dark areas), the 'Bunch of Bananas' (actually derived from the body and tail of the Indonesian Garuda bird), 'Sibi Saba' ('cushion cover', a four-part design that also includes a motif variously identified as a mat, or as an ostrich feather, but is in fact the female vulva with radiating

hair; hardly Indonesian, yet the overall configuration certainly is), and a design known variously as the 'Mask', the 'Canoe Prow', or the 'Back of the Tortoise'; and these continue in production at the present time. Designs representing West African interests in proverbs and in education included the 'Hands and Fingers', the 'Sword of Kingship', the postage stamps from Ghanaian ports; and these are likewise still in production. Indeed, the 'Hands and Fingers' design is currently printed by Brunnschweiler in sixteen different colourways.

🖎 Designs based on Egyptian motifs (for example mummies, pyramids, the ankh sign, the proto-dynastic Narmer palette) did not survive the second decade of this century, however; and, similarly, pictures of bridges, paths and trees in the Dutch countryside seem not to have got much further than an original printing (above). Additional designs were quickly added to the repertoire, such as the 'Staircase' and the 'Alphabet' invariably taking up a proverbial or educational significance (p.121); and at the present time, while the earliest surviving designs continue to be reworked into ever new configurations, newly thought-up designs continue to proliferate, particularly with the advent of factories and design studios located in West and Central Africa.

🖎 The Vlisco archives also show that from 1884 onwards, cloths were being printed in the Netherlands to the orders of German traders working in Mombasa, Dar es Salaam and Zanzibar, with designs that were quite different: with larger-scale motifs printed in brighter colours seemingly not at all like the hand-block designs brought to the East African coast from India and from which designs for *kanga* (literally 'Guinea Fowl') wrap-around skirts, now so characteristic of East Africa, were to develop.

🖎 It is, however, clear from the ABC archives (*ie* Brunnschweiler) that English developments took a rather different direction, though with the same end in view. In part this must have been because the Brown Flemming designs were not available to them as a source until his company was bought up by Grafton. Thus, in the engraving books of the Broad Oak printworks (Grafton was the retail outlet for Africa) we find that the first duplex wax print design was not sent out for engraving until 1909, and that the first designs making specific use of Gold Coast motifs such as bones and *adinkra* stamps, are from 1910-11. On the other hand, it is also in the Newton Bank archives that we find the first commemorative fancy prints, designed to the order of the United Africa Company. (Wax printing was not really a suitable medium for the more photographic imagery of the commemorative designs.) The earliest, dated 28 September 1928, is entitled 'Mammy', and depicts a woman who was presumably a market trader. The next is 'Nana Prempeh', the Asantehene, and is dated 29 October 1929; then an Ewe chief, Fiaga of Peki, 10 March 1931; then the Prince of Wales, 18 September 1931; and the commemorative potential of fancy prints was to prove of particular significance after 1945 and the movements towards Independence. Since then, fancy prints have continued to be used for commemorative and educational purposes; and the repertoire of both wax and fancy print designs has continued to expand.

This essay began with a story about a drummer who asked me to design a banner for him, and it has concluded with a rather more complicated story about a large number of people in Europe who, over the years, have been provided with the opportunities for work and art by people in Africa. An African patronage determined almost from the very outset what it wanted to see in these cloths, and it was an African patronage quick to recognise the advantage of someone else doing the work. Of course, with Independence and the wish to be self-sufficient, textile factories were set up in almost every country in West Africa, sometimes with the assistance of Britain or the Netherlands, and sometimes with the assistance of Indian or Chinese expertise. One inevitable consequence of this was the decline (but not the demise) in demand for European printed cloths, as the local factories began to produce both wax and fancy prints that were cheaper in price than the imported fabrics. Although a measure of revival of European involvement was provided by the opening of textile factories in Zaire, most of the design studios and printworks in the Netherlands and in England closed down, leaving Vlisco and ABC as the sole heirs to this tradition, surviving in the midst of a vast array of West African and East Asian competitors. Vlisco and ABC do, indeed, continue to thrive because they produce what has become a relatively costly and, to that extent, high-status cloth that also maintains its lead in terms of quality of design and technical skill, even while expecting any novel development to be copied in the local factories. As it happens, of course, the latest designs from Europe constitute, as they always have done, a response to the mediating influence of the local traders; and in any case, the local designers and producers do not merely replicate European designs, they also produce original designs, often on commission from the traders in the market-place, that effectively mediate local concerns that can be described, variously, as decorative, commemorative, proverbial, didactic and funerary.

Samples printed for German traders in East Africa c.1900.
Collection Vlisco, Helmond

United Africa Company Fancy Prints sample book
Earliest commemorative portrait yet identified, known as 'Mammy', 28 September 1929
Collection A. Brunnschweiler & Co., Hyde

United Africa Company Fancy Prints sample book
'Nana Prempeh' (the Asantehene), 29 October 1929
Collection A.Brunnschweiler & Co., Hyde

1 ❧ The exhibition on which this publication was based drew upon other material (especially the Venice and Alistair Lamb collection now in the Smithsonian Institution, Washington DC) only to fill those rare gaps in the existing British Museum collections.

2 ❧ For the Japanese tour, a new catalogue was written by John Mack and Christopher Spring.

3 ❧ Especially Jane Barbour, Renée Boser-Sarivaxevanis, Marion Johnson, Kate Kent, Brigitte Menzel, Roy Sieber; and Venice Lamb, who had published the first of her four books documenting the textiles of West Africa.

4 ❧ However, volume 11 of the journal *Textile History*, guest-edited by Dale Idiens and also published as *Textiles in Africa* (D.Idiens and K.Ponting, eds) in 1980, summarised the state of play at that time and included the first of the papers by Lisa Aronson concerning her research in Nigeria that would encourage a revision of this approach. Indeed, the ground of textile history in Africa was already beginning to shift away from an ethnographical purism. See Justine Cordwell and Ronald Schwarz, 1979; Fred Smith and Joanne Eicher, 1982; and Jean Borgatti, 1983; and then Lisa Aronson, 1992, and also the papers published the same year by the National Museum of African Art, Washington DC, *History, Design and Craft in West African Strip-woven Cloth*. African art studies were changing in any case (see, for example, Clementine Deliss, 1990).

5 ❧ Yet the very contrast between the old and the new, or between this and that kind of development, can be problematic. It implies a classification on the basis of verifiable criteria, and while there may be nothing wrong with that provided we are agreed as to the nature and motivation of those criteria, the danger is that one falls into the discreditable Eurocentric habit of classifying alien peoples and practices as if they were butterflies or birds' eggs. Of course, without the ability to classify things, there could be no art, no language and no humanity; and provided we understand that any sorting out here is provisional, that we do not make a fetish out of taxonomy, that what ought to matter is not whether I can fit things into a scheme of my own invention, but rather the categorical procedures inherent in the contextual circumstances of a given particular local situation, then we can proceed.

6 ❧ See David Hammond-Tooke and Anitra Nettleton, 1989.

7 ❧ See Maude Wahlman and Eyinna Chuta, 1979.

8 ❧ See Jill Salmons, 1980.

9 ❧ See Tonye Erekosina and Joanne Eicher, 1981.

10 ❧ See Tavy Aherne, 1992.

11 ❧ See John Picton and John Mack, 1989, and Irene Emery, 1966.

12 ❧ Especially the idea of the artist as genius (*ie* imbued with a *djinn*, a pre-Islamic Arabian tutelary deity) inscribed within a nineteenth-century romanticism.

13 ❧ They probably derive from the Igbo 'Maiden spirit' masquerades. See Jean Borgatti, 1979, John Boston, 1960, Herbert Cole and Chike Aniakor, 1986.

14 ❧ 'But a problem of identity was inherent in their very situation . . . Matters such as names and dress acquired an immense symbolic importance . . . Some adopted Nigerian dress as a symbol of African identity . . .', E.Isichei, 1983, p.341; see also M.J.C.Echeruo, 1977, p.39.

15 ❧ This is at least implied by the photographs of the period, see for example Agneta Pallinder, 1990, p.19.

16 ❧ This is the area once dominated by the kindom of Oyo-Ile until its defeat by the Fulani *jihad* in the second quarter of the nineteenth century.

17 ❧ John Picton and John Mack, *African Textiles*, 1989, p.110, illustrates a green cotton and yellow rayon Yoruba cloth purchased in Asante which confirms that 'silk' float-weave embellishments were already well established in the period between 1918 and 1939. Indeed, J.D.Clarke, 1938 noted that coloured silk yarn had been available in Ilorin from around 1933; but that cannot have been the origin of the float-weave technique as earlier evidence for it is available in cloths attributed to various locations in the middle Niger region. Ann O'Hear in her study of Ilorin weaver Yahaya Kalu Olabintan (*c*.1890-1982) concluded that, while he was reckoned to be the finest weaver in his day and was evidently the most experimental in his use of weft floats, he may have popularised the technique but it is unlikely that he invented it.

18 ❧ Elisha Renne reports (publication forthcoming 1995) that in the Ekiti districts of eastern Yoruba 'weaving is now considered a viable economic alternative to teaching, a common occupation for women with some secondary school education'. Yoruba textiles have become so much a focus for recent and current research (*eg* Carolyn Keyes-Adenaike, Duncan Clarke, Pat Oyelola, Elisha Renne, Norma Wolf) that one can now hope for a more definitive account than is yet available.

19 ❧ See John Picton, 1992.

20 ❧ See *The Nigerian Times*, 15-28 April 1995, New York.

21 ❧ I am relieved to find this hypothesis confirmed by Carolyn Keyes-Adenaike in her PhD thesis on *adire*.

22 ❧ Carolyn Keyes-Adenaike suggests that starch-resist would have commenced about 1910.

23 ❧ See Jane Barbour, 1971, John Picton and John Mack, 1989, George Jackson, 1971.

24 ❧ See Nike Olaniyi-Davies, 1991, p.20.

25 ❧ See Toyin Oguntona, 1986, p.76. The resemblance of *kampala* methods (folding or crumpling and tieing, spattering or printing with molten wax) to dyeing in Sierra Leone will be obvious. See M.Wahlman and E.Chuta, 1979.

26 ❧ Oshogbo is a Yoruba town where from the early 1960s onwards an annual series of workshops has been held for people who have not had access to art practice within the educational system. See Ulli Beier, 1991.

27 ❧ We still know very little of the histories of these two technologies; and the facts that the same yarns are used on each, that in the 1960s one could see patterns and motifs developed on one as a source of developments in the other, and that women in many areas are abandoning the one in favour of the other, are about the only obvious points of contact.

28 ❧ For data concerning Ijebu and Akwete, and Ewe involvement in the Niger Delta and southern Igbo areas we are indebted to Lisa Aronson's research: see 1992, 1989, 1984, 1982, 1980a, 1980b.

29 ❧ There is also the occasional work such as the late fourteenth-century brass jug, now in the Mediaeval Department of the British Museum, that was removed by the British army in 1896 from a shrine in the royal mausoleum of the kings of Asante.

30 ❧ See Peggy Gilfoy, 1988, p.26.

31 ❧ Indeed, I have suggested elsewhere that the distinctive features of Asante weaving could have arisen in the attempt to reproduce a weft-faced patterning with a loom set up to produce an essentially warp-faced cloth. An intriguing parallel to this hypothesis is provided by the necessity of evolving a double-warp structure in order to reproduce the characteristic features of Asante weaving on a horizontal broadloom in Dutch factories, as also at the Kumasi cultural centre in modern Ghana.

32 ❧ See Venice Lamb, 1975.

33 ❧ See Venice Lamb, 1975, p.104.

34 ❧ Cotton is not a forest product, and in any case it can be woven faster than it can be spun (a production bottleneck that in Britain was at the heart of the Industrial Revolution).

35 ❧ See Venice Lamb, 1975, p.106.

36 ❧ Since then *adwinasa* have not been woven in this manner: the name persisted for cloths embellished throughout with float-weave pattern, but with increasing repetition of a smaller number of motifs.

37 ❧ The three pairs of heddles are *asatia* used for the warp-faced areas of the cloth, *asanan* used for the weft-faced and float-weave patterning, and *asasia* enabling a twilled float-weave.

38 ❧ See Herbert Cole and Doran Ross, 1977.

39 ❧ See Venice Lamb, 1975, p.165.

40 ❧ See Venice Lamb, 1975; Merrick Posnansky, 1992.

41 ❧ See Venice Lamb, 1975, p.95.

42 ❧ Kathleen Bickford, 1994, Bea Brommer, 1989, Susan Domowitz, 1992, W.T. Kroese, 1976, Ruth Nielsen, 1979, Christopher Steiner, 1985.

43 ❧ As reported by Margaret Hickson, formerly of the design studio of Arthur Brunnschweiler & Co., Hyde.

44 ❧ Mrs Ruth Cobbinah, from whom I recently purchased textiles in Kumasi market, Ghana, distinguished between wax prints, Java prints and fancy prints. The latter were the very cheapest quality produced in China, whereas Java prints were rather better quality and printed in Ghana. Her wax prints were from Nigeria and Ivory Coast, as she could no longer afford to stock Dutch or English wax. The term Java print originates in printed copies of Indonesian batiks producd by firms such as Vlisco before the developments of Previnaire and Haarlem.

45 ❧ Brian Anderton, unpublished papers, Arthur Brunnschweiler & Co.

46 ❧ See W.T.Kroese, 1976, pp.35-46: the emphasis Kroese places on this was rather discounted by C.H. Krantz, now retired from Vlisco, but still regarded as the authority on the history of wax prints; but it cannot be without some significance.

47 ❧ See W.T.Kroese, 1976, pp.47-55.

48 ❧ The names quoted for these designs are as given at Vlisco and ABC.

Factory-printed cotton
Obra Tese Nkosua, Ghana
c.1995
Collection
John and Susan Picton

MANDINKA

SENEGAL
Dakar• •Thiès
GUINEA
BISSAU

SIERRA LEONE

MALI

Niger
DOGON
Ségou
Bamako• •Djenné

IVORY
COAST
Abidjan•

GHANA
Accra•

TOGO
BENIN

Niamey•

Ouagadougou•

NIGER

NIGERIA

Benue

Lagos•

CAMEROON

CAIRO is labeled Cairo•

EGYPT

Nile

Khartoum•

SUDAN

KENYA
•Eldoret
•Nairobi
Pate
Lamu
•Mombasa

Congo

ZAIRE

Kisangani•

SUNDI-KONGO

•Kinshasa

KUBA

TANZANIA

Dar es Salaam• ZANZIBAR

ZAMBIA •Kabwe
Lusaka• Zambezi
Kafue• L.
Kariba
•Harare
ZIMBABWE
•Bulawayo

MALAWI

MERINA
Arivonimamo• •Antananarivo
BETSILEO

TSONGA
TRANSVAAL
LOBEDU
Pretoria•
Johannesburg•
NATAL
NDEBELE

MADAGASCAR

SOUTH AFRICA

Cape Town•

•Durban

XHOSA

Grahamstown•

XHOSA   Peoples

NATAL   Countries and regions

Durban   Cities/towns/villages

0   500   1000 miles

0   500   1000   1500   2000 kilometres

Elizabeth Harney

THE TAPESTRIES OF THIÈS:
WOVEN IMAGES OF NEGRITUDE

❧ In 1966, Senegal hosted the *Premier festival mondial des arts nègres* in Dakar to celebrate African artistic expression. This festival featured a plethora of musical, theatrical and dance performances as well as exhibitions of visual arts from past and present. Léopold Sédar Senghor, the first President of Senegal and an eminent poet-philosopher, used this occasion to introduce his philosophy of *Négritude* to an international audience. Negritude was essentially a theory of racial belonging, based upon the existence of a shared *âme nègre*, or black soul, which sought to define a place for the black man worldwide. By the time Senghor spoke of Negritude to his audience in 1966, it had been a locus of debate for several decades, finding its roots in an ideological movement of young black students from the French colonies who gathered in 1930s Paris to discuss issues of colonialism and identity. Aimé Césaire, Martiniquan poet and statesman, was the first to coin the term,[1] broadly defining it as the 'simple recognition of the fact of being black, and the acceptance of this fact, of our destiny as black people, of our history, and of our culture'.[2] Years later Senghor gave his own definition of Negritude, a concept which for him developed from a personal philosophy into a blueprint for forging a nationalist and pan-African post-Independence identity and aesthetic. 'Negritude is quite simply the assembly of the values of the black civilisation. It is not racism, it is culture.'[3]

❧ In his theory of racial belonging, Senghor attributed certain characteristics to Africans which, in many cases, mirrored European stereotypes of the continent and her peoples. Drawing on the writings of European ethnographers, Senghor co-opted many of their visions of the 'primitive' and reinterpreted them as virtues and values of African cultures. Thus, the *âme nègre* was said to be emotive, spiritual, expressive and rhythmic. Furthermore, Senghor encouraged the development of a new visual vocabulary through which to express this shared soul. This aesthetic combined the technology of Europe, in the form of easel painting in oils, gouaches, and Gobelin wool tapestries, with a vocabulary of African-inspired themes and motifs. The works of this so-called *École de Dakar* focused on images of an exotic Africa, either idyllic in its villages, lively in its markets, or mystical in its bush. The motifs of masks, sculpted figures, incised combs, ceremonial vessels and textile patterning were drawn from throughout the continent and mixed with invented forms. Senghor's sanction and promotion of the arts defined a place for the Senegalese artist in his/her new nation as both an agent of development and, perhaps more importantly, as an ambassador for Senegal to the rest of the world.

❧ In 1965, as part of the institutionalisation of his cultural programme, Senghor inaugurated the Manufactures Sénégalaises des Arts Décoratifs (MSAD) in Thiès, a Gobelin-styled tapestry centre whose productions, in the decade to follow, came to symbolise the *École de Dakar*. He invited Papa Ibra Tall to direct this new centre and remained himself an active participant in the institution, heading the special committee for the selection of designs and using the finished products as official state gifts. These woven images became emblems of a free and creative new nation. Both Senghor and Tall regarded them as public-orientated and accessible arts which could illustrate the important role of culture in the development process. Tall insisted, 'We are convinced that it is by the decorative and monumental arts that we will reach the ideal of all democratic civilisations: to immerse the people in art, an ideal which ancient Africa had achieved.'[4] It is ironic that these tapestries became the most expensive of the arts: one which only could be purchased by the government or foreigners. Thiès tapestries generally were not collected by ordinary citizens, much less seen by them on a daily basis.[5]

❧ In the 1950s, Tall had trained as an architecture student in Paris where he had enjoyed close ties to many members of the Negritude 'movement'. He regarded his directorship at MSAD as an opportunity to expand his support for Negritude and to develop a new vocabulary to express his Africanness. He recalls:

So at the time it was a question of creating for myself an artistic language which seemed to me to belong to Africa and to Senegal. I concluded that art was universal but that it was necessary for there to be particularities that one had to transcend to achieve this universality. So I thought that I couldn't imitate what the French were doing. I was completely outside that tradition. Therefore, I thought that it was necessary for me to construct a completely new language. I was inspired by the theory of Negritude which back then, you must recall, was unique. Wole Soyinka didn't yet exist and the other theoreticians of the day were economic theoreticians – Nkrumah had an economic theory not cultural. So, those of us who wanted to create something autonomous, belonging to and reflecting just us, had little to inspire us but Negritude. . .[6]

❧ Tall sent four students to train in France at the weaving workshops of Aubusson and Beauvais, and imported dyed wools from Belgium and Holland and looms from France.[7] Unlike local traditions of weaving which were male-dominated, tapestries at Thiès were woven by both women and men. The students at the École des Arts submitted small painted tapestry designs. During its early days, the workshop had an artist-in-residence programme in which painters/tapestry makers such as Alioune Badiane, Ousmane Faye, Mamadou Niang, Mamadou Wade and others, worked.

Their designs were, for the most part, very decorative, with interweaving and intricate, colourful patterns. Some seemed to be modelled after those of Tall himself, whose works featured elongated figures, occupying shallow space, and a mass of sinuous lines. Others featured highly geometric, architectonic figures, based on the sculpted wooden figures and masks of the African continent. The limitations of this weaving technology resulted in compositions with flat, large tracts of colour which were highly geometric and 'semi-abstract'.[8] These compositional qualities have often served as markers of the *École de Dakar* style.

Once selected, these models were transferred to a grid and enlarged tenfold to measure about 203 x 254 cm. The colours were numbered to produce an easy pattern for the weavers to follow. In the late 1980s and early 1990s, artists received 100,000 CFA (about £270 then) for their original designs. Four editions could be made from the original model. If further ones were commissioned, the MSAD gave the artists a percentage of the sale. In the 1970s, under the directorship of Alioune Badiane, the number of editions increased to six.

The heyday of Thiès was in the late 1960s and 1970s, when it enjoyed strong government patronage. By 1980, the current President, Abdou Diouf, had replaced President Senghor and began to redirect the government's priorities away from cultural to economic development. Although the government remains the largest patron of Senegalese arts, it has drastically reduced this support. Thiès presently operates at a greatly diminished capacity, producing only several tapestries a year. While there is talk of privatisation there seems little possibility for this

endeavour in the aftermath of the currency devaluation of 1994.

The importance of Thiès tapestries lies not simply in their physical and ideological legacy,[9] but also in the new arts it inspired. So strong was this legacy that many artists currently at work in Senegal still refer to its productions in their works. A prime example is the work of muralist El Sy who, in protest at the rigid canonisation of the *École de Dakar* and the expense of imported materials for the Thiès tapestries, paints on rice sacks (found in every Senegalese home), displaying them as one would a tapestry. On a different conceptual level, the designs of Aissa Dione, a Senegalese artist who has built a successful design business using local weaving traditions and pan-African themes, reflects the legacy of Thiès, and the importance of fabrics in the cultural consciousness of the nation.

1 Aimé Césaire, 1939
2 Aimé Césaire as quoted in Abiola Irele, 1977, p.1
3 Léopold Sédar Senghor, Lecture at Oxford University, 26 October 1961. 'La Négritude est, tout simplement, l'ensemble des valeurs de civilisation du monde noir. Il n'est pas racisme, il est culture.' (Author's translation.)
4 Papa Ibra Tall, 'Situation de l'Artiste Nègro-Africain Contemporain' in *Art Nègre et Civilisation de l'Universel*, Dakar, Nouvelles Éditions Africaines, 1975, no.93 'Nous sommes convaincus que c'est par les arts décoratifs et monumentaux que nous réaliserons l'idéal de toute civilisation démocratique: faire de l'art un bain du peuple, idéal que la vieille Afrique avait atteint.' (Author's translation.)
5 Their cost began at 400,000 CFA (about £600), figures from 1990.
6 Papa Ibra Tall, personal interview, Thiès, Senegal, May 1994. (Author's translation.)
7 Originally, the imported looms were of the basse-loom type. Then, in the 1980s, eight haute-looms were added.
8 Ima Ebong, 1991, pp.198-209.
9 Especially through travelling exhibitions such as *Art sénégalais d'aujourd'hui*, which began at the Grand Palais (Paris, 1974) and toured, in a smaller form, around North America.

Mohamadou Zulu M'Baye
Couple d'enfants
Wool tapestry, 1992
Collection Manufactures Sénégalaises des Arts Décoratifs, Thiès

Papa Ibra Tall
Couple Royal
Wool tapestry, 1966

Pauline Duponchel

BOGOLAN: FROM SYMBOLIC MATERIAL
TO NATIONAL EMBLEM

❧ Since the beginning of the 1980s a change in taste has taken place in the capital of Mali, which is more than just a question of fashion. Mud-dyed fabric has gradually become very important in fashion as well as in interior decoration, and the spectacular rise in its popularity originated in the fine arts. Yet up until then, these Bamana cloths had been despised, stigmatised by associations with rural garments and animist practices in contrast to the grand gowns worn in the city and Islam. This essay sets out to explain the stages in this revival.

❧ To understand the situation in Mali, however, we have to go back a bit further than the 1980s. When the country gained its independence in 1960 cultural weeks were organised regionally and the women from the villages around Djenné were employed to decorate the *bogolan* costumes to be worn by the dance troupes and had to mass produce them very quickly. They still talk about it today, openly admitting that they did not have time to make them carefully and skilfully. To speed up their output they increased the size of their tools and their motifs. Consequently what was initially a self-sufficient economic activity gradually became work that brought in a small income. Thus towards the end of the 1960s there were two forms of *bogolan*: one deeply rooted in village life and traditional practice, and the other intended to enhance the prestige of the regions each year in theatrical performances staged in the capital.

❧ In 1974, a young Malian artist in Bamako by the name of Kandioura Coulibaly started studying at the Institut National des Arts (INA); on graduating four years later he submitted a final thesis entitled '*Bogolan*, a traditional technique for dying cloth with vegetable dyes'. He and the artist Lamine Sidibé share the distinction of having dared to appropriate for artistic purposes a technique of decoration that had been a female province. From 1978 Lamine Sidibé, along with other instructors, started organising workshops teaching *bogolan* techniques in camps of pioneers (a youth movement similar to the Scouts).

❧ At the same time Seydou Nourou Doumbia, working under the name 'Chris Seydou' as the first African fashion designer in Paris, could not resist using a *bogolan* as a draped scarf and designing a head-dress of *bogolan* at a fashion show where he was presenting his winter collection in 1979. This was a symbolic event and a turning point in his career; after returning to Africa in 1981 he continued to enhance the status of the traditional textiles of West Africa and dared to cut up lengths of cloth used for rituals or which had previously been worn exclusively by just one social class.

❧ At the beginning of the 1980s members of the group subsequently known as Bogolan Kasobane carried out research into *bogolan*, learning the technique and improving upon it

at Markala in the region of Ségou. Using only this technique the group painted works as a team of six, participating in film-making, stage productions and interior decoration by creating costumes or sets. They were the main protagonists behind the revival described here.

❧ In 1981 the painter Ismaël Diabate, drawing tutor at the *lycée* in Markala, was taught the technique in a week by Kandioura Coulibaly and Souleymane Goro, two members of the group, while Lamine Sidibé showed him the plants and the places along the river Niger where he could find earth that was suitably rich in ferric oxide. Lamine Sidibé also taught him how to soak his materials and, most importantly, the tricky technique of laundering them. He thus discovered how to produce deep blacks and luminous whites. Ismaël then reworked some of his pictures, treating them with clay. Initially very close to the decorative style of the artists in the Bogolan Kasobane group, he eventually freed his work of all other influences.

❧ Thus first from the women and then from one another, artists gradually learnt the rudiments of this skill for which the raw materials could be found in nature. Clearly the self-sufficiency with which *bogolan* can be produced takes account of the economic difficulties of those making it and the problems of procuring supplies, but that does not explain everything. Very quickly, while retaining the fundamental recipe, they felt a need to diversify the support materials used, moving on from lengths of hand-spun and hand-woven cotton to cretonne, percale, voile and even wood.

❧ In 1988, Ali Dolo, Hama Goro and Rokiatou Sow, who had also studied at the INA and belonged to the cultural co-operative run by Alpha Oumar Konare, President of Mali, opened the Jamana workshop. They create works using liquid mud on cretonne canvases and have even gone so far as to apply earth onto wood.

❧ In 1990 Chris Seydou returned to Bamako, and at every subsequent fashion parade provoked astonishment and, ultimately, enthusiasm for this once despised material. He flouted every convention, showing *bogolan* made into mini-skirts or bustiers, as large berets or full-fitting coats and even as a fitted suit worn by the President's wife Adam Ba Konare for the opening of a film festival in Marseilles in 1993. The annual festival of Malian television features an eagerly anticipated fashion show to which Chris Seydou contributed in 1992, 1993 and 1994. *Bogolan* was all the rage; Seydou cut the dyed material intelligently, respecting the graphic design of the motifs and mixing some of them in a humorous way. In 1991, with the help of the Bogolan Kasobane group and the Jamana workshop, he designed all the costumes for the Mande opera *Waramba* staged by Souleymane Koly. In 1992, using designs produced by Chris Seydou's team, the ITEMA

Bogolan ('mudcloth')
Discharge-dyed narrow-strip cotton cloth
Mali, rainy season 1991
Private Collection

textile company (Industrie Textile du Mali) manufactured *bogolan pagnes* (wrap-around skirts) exclusively for him to use in his ready-to-wear range. Whether in South Africa in 1992 or Abidjan, Ouagadougou, Paris (for the Salon du Prêt-à-Porter) and Accra in 1993, everywhere he went he imposed the use of *bogolan*.

❀ Meanwhile in 1992, Aminata Dramane Traore opened a cultural showplace known as 'SANTORO' with the exclusive right to sell the latest textiles created by the Bogolan Kasobane group and the Jamana workshop; these decorate entrance doors and the backs of armchairs and upright chairs which are also intended for the offices of the various ministries. The place is like a laboratory in which Aminata alters the interior decoration, adding a picture or continuing a product line in accordance with how they are received. Customers understand that this special approach is designed to enhance the value of Mali's cultural heritage.

❀ In 1992 a Malian industrialist called Cheick Oumar Diao gave the Ségou textile factory COMATEX (Compagnie Malienne des Textiles) the design for a *bogolan* which was to be printed in black and blue. This *bogolan pagne* made of factory-produced cotton was subsequently launched and in spite of its poor quality has been selling ever since. In 1994 he tried to have the pattern produced in Mali on other support materials such as linen and voile in order to create coordinated fabrics, offering Chris Seydou exclusive rights to these. Unfortunately, however, Chris Seydou died in March 1994 and it will be the Nigerian fashion designer, Alphadi, who will launch this line with *bogolan* produced in a range of colours, including black, blue, green and even pink.

❀ Marine Biras of the Galerie des Textiles in Paris suggests that a number of factors contributed to the growing fashionability of *bogolan* there towards the end of the 1980s. The ecology movement, the fact that people were tired of the uniformity of factory-made goods, and first and foremost, the presence of such companies as ETNI-TECHNI, ACCOSTAGE and SANTORO at interior decoration exhibitions in 1993 presenting *bogolan* designed to appeal to the taste of European customers – all these factors stimulated the increasing demand for these cloths. At the start of the 1994 school year in Bamako, schoolchildren received little exercise books with covers printed with a *bogolan* design in black and yellow or white, blue, green. These were distributed by Aliou Tomota, a young printer and industrialist.

❀ At FESPACO in 1995 Kandioura Coulibaly, Boubacar Doumbia and Baba Fallo Keita won the prizes for the best costumes and the best sets for Cheick Oumar Sissoko's film *Guimba*. *Bogolan* features extensively in it.

❀ In Bamako there is not a single artist who has not experimented with this material nor a single student or woman who does not wear one. In Paris in magazines (*Marie-Claire Maison*, *Elle Déco*, *Maison Française*, the Trois Suisses catalogue etc.) and at exhibitions (*Au fil de la parole* at the Fondation Dapper in 1995) *bogolan* are featured and the price of *bogolan* cloths in commercial outlets fluctuates between 200Ffr and 700Ffr depending on the season. Whether in American films (*Point Break*, *Single White Female*, *The Fugitive*) or advertising (Gervais) the black and white graphics of *bogolan* make an impression, slily turning up in unexpected places. For the black American population of the United States *bogolan*, like *kente*, is a symbol of belonging to African culture.

❀ In Mali it can be confidently stated that in ten years the skill of making *bogolan* has become the emblem of a generation and even the expression of Malian national identity.

Translated from the French by Spalter Translations

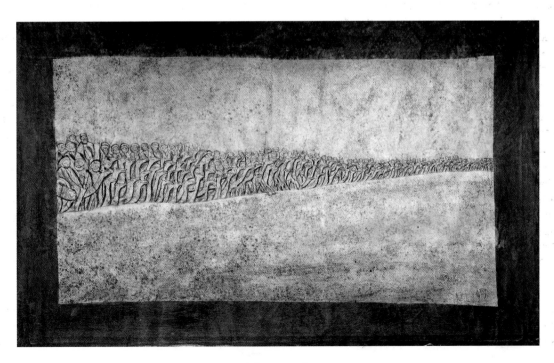

Alfousseini Kelly
La Traversée du Désert (Crossing the Desert)
Bogolan ('mudcloth') discharge-dyed canvas, Mali, 1993
Collection the artist

David Heathcote

ASPECTS OF EMBROIDERY
IN NIGERIA

🖐 Embroidery plays an important part in Nigerian textiles and the examples of men's gowns that are included in the exhibition illustrate significant aspects. A number of these gowns were collected among the Hausa of northern Nigeria (pp.72-6), and a further gown from among the Nupe, who live farther to the south. The most modern gown is Hausa (p.76). The embroidery on it was made with a Cornely-type sewing machine, and the design's name, *Yar Kumasi* ('Daughter of Kumasi'), indicates that Ghana was the source from which it came to Hausaland in the present century.

🖐 Three of the gowns bear an embroidery design for which there is evidence of widespread use in Nigeria since the mid-nineteenth century, but whose origins date to a much earlier period. It is known as 'Eight Knives' (Hausa: *aska takwas*). The name refers to eight pointed wedge shapes on the gown's left side (opposite). 'Eight Knives' was probably a development of a less elaborate, but in some respects closely related, scheme known as 'Two Knives' (*aska biyu*). Though there is no evidence for the first appearance of these two designs, museum specimens indicate that they originated in a decorative development of structural

features incorporated as strengtheners on men's gowns, and that this was accompanied by the addition of motifs adopted by the Hausa from the Islamic world.

🖐 Subsequently, while maintaining their basic underlying scheme, the 'Two Knives' and the 'Eight Knives' designs were spread over an increasingly broad area of the gowns they decorated, progressing through a process of gradual enlargement to a stage of considerably elaborated stitching. This expansion of the embroidery on men's gowns suggests a situation of increasing economic prosperity, and a desire on the part of the embroiderers' patrons to signal their wealth and status.

🖐 Another feature of the development of these designs is the way in which modifications of them have passed back and forth between Hausa, Nupe, Yoruba and other embroiderers. This exchange of decorative ideas is indicated in the Hausa name for one of their own variations of 'Eight Knives', still remembered in the 1970s by old embroiderers. The Hausa term for it is *Yar Ilori* ('Daughter of Ilorin'), Ilorin being a large town in Yorubaland. Further evidence of cross-cultural influence occurs in the embroidery on one of the gowns made in Kano. This embodies

Alhaji Sanni embroidering *Yayin Sharif mai Wata*
(Sharif style with Crescent Moon) design
outside his house, Kano, 1974

Machine embroiderers working on
Yar Kumasi ('Daughter of Kumasi') design
1976

modifications made to the Hausa 'Eight Knives' design by a Borno embroiderer, Sharif, and later additions, including a crescent-moon motif, by Alhaji Sanni, a Hausa embroiderer. Sanni's name for this variation of his was *Yayin Sharif mai Wata* ('The Sharif Style with a Crescent Moon'). It was Sanni who drew the design onto the cloth of the gown, and he also executed some of the embroidery. Precise evidence of Sanni's creative contribution is by good fortune preserved in a working drawing he made for it (below). He kept this drawing in his house along with others, employing some of them in the manner of a pattern book by showing them to prospective clients. These drawings provide a rare insight into the way in which an embroiderer, working within the constraints of a restrictive decorative format in the 1950s and 1960s, was examining ways in which he might modify well-established designs in order to arrive at something new which did not flout accepted conventions.

Important among the men who have been instrumental in developing hand embroidery designs in West Africa are those who acquired skills in calligraphy and drawing through a study of the Qur'an, men who were working in a situation where there was increasing contact with the Islamic world and in which, as already indicated, embroidered clothing was an important status symbol. If we also take into account the anxiety that has existed in West Africa, as elsewhere, to obtain protection against 'the evil eye', it is understandable that some of these men, with their skills in writing and drawing, and access to what many would have considered the magic of the Qur'an, would have been in demand for their ability to make protective as well as decorative contributions to clothing. Did such demands in any way affect the development of the embroidery?

There is, in fact, ample evidence for the existence of charms associated with West African gowns. Some gowns have small leather packets sewn into them that enclose papers bearing drawn motifs and accurate, or confused, quotations from the Qur'an. One such gown was offered to me in a Hausa market during the Nigerian civil war in the late 1960s. There are others on which writing and signs have been inscribed directly onto the cloth of the garment. An unusual type of Hausa gown made in Kano, and known as *shabka* is illustrated on p.76. Although the possible association of the *shabka* with charms may at first sight appear unlikely, it does have a distinct connection with them. While there appears to be little doubt that every *shabka* – and related types of gown – that I have examined was of West African manufacture, the *shabka* is nevertheless on record as having been worn in the past particularly by Arabs. This in itself may have endowed it with a certain aura. Certainly it has, as we shall see, distinct, even though distant, connections with charm garments and, specifically, with Hausa versions of the Qur'an. The *shabka* included in the exhibition is, typically, embroidered on both the front and the back with an elaborate arrangement of squares and circles. Each embroidered circle has first been cut out of the cloth, and the resulting edges have then been folded back to create a gap which the embroiderer has filled with a form of needle-weaving. Considering the extraordinary amount of labour needed for embroidery of this type, and the fact that lightweight clothing has now become more fashionable, it is not surprising that the *shabka* is no longer commissioned.

Two especially distinguishing features of the *shabka* on display are worth noting. Firstly, its overall decorative scheme bears a striking resemblance to certain West African charms drawn on paper, and which include prominent squares and circles set out in arrangements that have similarities with the decoration on the *shabka*. Such charms would have been derived from various African and other Islamic sources. Secondly, the arrangement of the decoration on this gown bears a startling resemblance to that on a Muslim, fifteenth-century talismanic undershirt from India (now in the Royal Museum of Scotland in Edinburgh 1982.3) on which prayers and chapters from the Qur'an, and the Muslim profession of faith, are inscribed. The calligraphy has been carried out within a design of squares and circles resembling the layout on certain West African charm papers as well as that on the *shabka*.

While recognising that the association between protective charms and the embroidery may never have been more than marginal, there is nevertheless a clear, if far-flung, connection between the Indian undershirt, a number of African charms drawn on paper, and the Hausa *shabka*. Furthermore, although the *shabka* in the exhibition is devoid of writing, it nevertheless bears, within many of its circular, embroidered motifs, linear configurations for which one can find matching parallels in Hausa versions of the Qur'an. This, together with other aspects of embroidery in Nigeria, indicates that there is scope for further investigation.

Alhaji Sanni
Yayin Sharif mai Wata (Sharif style with Crescent Moon)
Working drawing for embroidery design
c.1965
Private collection

Pat Oyelola

TEXTILE MARKETS IN NIGERIA:
A DIARY

🐦 *10 January 1995*
I made two trips to Oje market in Ibadan, on 24 December 1994 and 9 January 1995. Most of the cloth on sale was cotton with discreet lurex stripes. The sources of the cotton are mills in Ado Ekiti, Lagos and Kano, ascertained from the labels on hanks of thread on sale in the market. Lurex, sold on reels under the trade name 'Brightex', comes from Japan. Only two traders in the market sold 'silk' *aso oke*. The 'silk' is in fact 'Hafrayon' made by Haffar in Mushin, Lagos. The decorative effects on the *aso oke* on sale are produced by stripes of varying colours and thicknesses. I did not see any with 'brocaded' designs, holes or floating threads (except in the second-hand section), but lots of lemon-yellow cotton *aso oke* in combination with black stripes/gold lurex stripes/silver lurex stripes, or 'shot' weft-wise with silver.

🐦 *29 January 1995*
Yesterday, 28 January 1995, I went to Itoku market, the main market for cloth in Abeokuta. There was very little indigo *adire* on sale. I saw stencilled designs on poplin at N420 (Naira) for five yards. Designs included the cassava leaf pattern, stylised cowrie shells, keys and straight lines – each design executed all over the cloth in neatly organised rows. Each cloth featured one design only.
🐦 What was very much in evidence was 'brocade', otherwise known as 'Guinea brocade' or 'Guinea', in a rainbow array of colours further enriched with patterns obtained by tie-dyeing or stitching or wax batik, all techniques used on the old indigo *adire*. The equivalent of 'brocade' in an English context is 'damask' as formerly used for tablecloths. The cheaper-quality brocades are made in Nigeria and China, the silkier, finer ones in Europe. Those I saw in the market belonged to the cheaper range. The designs woven into the brocade by the manufacturer were mostly floral in character, but there were some geometrics. The added patterns bore no relation to the ground-design. The cassava leaf appeared frequently as a stencilled design framed by rows of dots and repeated in lines all over the surface. There were many freehand, wax batik designs – loosely executed swirls, curves, lines, triangles and ellipses; also some very dainty, stitched designs – rows of scallops. In addition, there were cloths with tie-dyed 'sun-bursts' in a row down the middle.
🐦 Brocade could also be bought in pieces designed to be made into a *boubou*, a long, loose dress with a curved neckline. The patterns in this case were placed strategically for cutting out the neck and sewing up the sides. The *boubou* cloth was often two-tone, *eg* purple ground with a broad yellow border and yellow geometric designs on the body.
🐦 While in the market I took a quick look at *ankara* – prints.

Cotton prints with a polished surface are very popular now – the sheen comes off at the first wash! Since wax prints were always regarded as superior, somone has hit on a sure-fire trademark printed all along the selvedge of the cloth – 'Guaranteed Imi-wax'. (The concept of a guaranteed imitation is very interesting!) Many of these prints have geometric designs: the same design is frequently executed in two or three different colour combinations.

🐦 *7 February 1995*
Cloth is woven and sold both at the weaving cooperative and through individual enterprises in Akwete. The cloth is made for local women but is also bought by expatriates. Local women buy and wear cloths in pairs to make two wrappers draped around the waist, one on top of the other. Prices range from N2000 to N4000 for a pair of wrappers. However, they can be ordered singly or even in narrower widths. The standard width is approximately 116 cm. A weaver named 'Blessing' travels regularly to Port Harcourt and weaves to order. She also brings ready-woven cloth to sell. Her own work is of very high quality. When she gets a large order, she sub-contracts.

🐦 *Ibadan, 14 February 1995*
The company 'Afprint' was originally owned by Germans, then by Japanese and now by Indians who are part of the Chanrai group. Raw cotton is obtained from Nigeria, Benin, Togo and Israel, and

*Oba (king) and Olori (consort) of Gbongan
at their coronation, July 1989
The Oba (right) wears hand-embroidered damask gown
and plumed white beaded crown; the Olori, gown
with recurring crown motif.*

is spun and woven in Lagos in a mill owned by the same company. The designers are Nigerian, as are the workers on the factory floor. The management is Indian. The designers, trained in-house, used to be sent to Holland and Germany for training, but this stopped fifteen years ago. No art-school graduates are employed. The designers were copying from samples of English and Dutch prints (the mill manager also had a collection of samples of Indonesian prints). He said he sometimes suggested ideas for original designs.

🦋 Afprint prints seventy designs per month of which approximately 25 per cent are new designs – the rest are repeats of fast-selling designs. Each design is produced in a run of 25,000 metres in four or five colourways. Distribution is mainly through Kewalam's, but UAC and CFAO also distribute under their own labels, even though the cloth is printed by Afprint, which distributes all over Nigeria, taking note of regional colour preferences (red and yellow are favourites east of the Niger, for example). The company aims for the working-class market but also produces some higher quality branded goods made with superior cotton on superior looms.

🦋 Distributors have a great influence over the type of designs produced. They may even bring samples of designs to be copied. Designs containing familiar motifs found in the old Dutch and English prints are very popular. There is a copyright on English and Dutch designs, but this is disregarded. Sometimes a name is attached to a design by the purchasers; when this happens, the cloth becomes a best-seller. The name does not necessarily bear any direct relation to the design.

Fancy print cotton textile
Printed by Afprint, Nigeria
1995

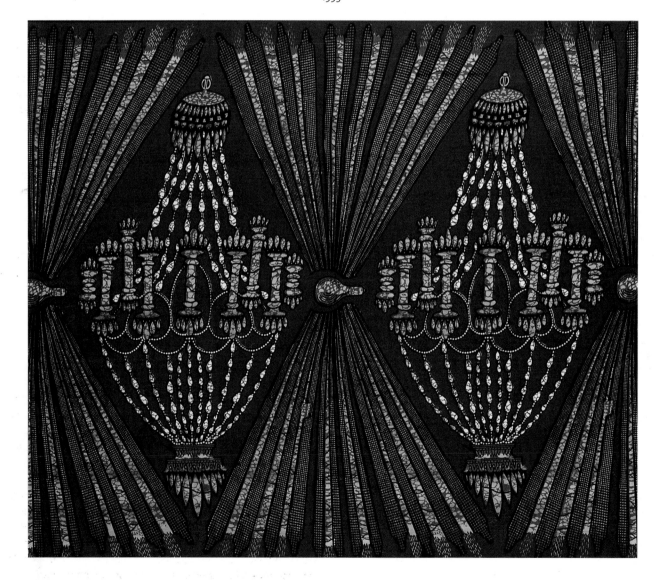

Atta Kwami

TEXTILE DESIGN IN GHANA:
EXTRACTS FROM A REPORT

The Gold Coast became Ghana in 1957 and embarked on a programme of industrialisation to minimise the country's reliance on imported goods. In 1965 the first textile factory, Ghana Textile Manufacturing Company (GTMC), was set up at Tema, Ghana's largest port, for the production of printed fabrics known as 'mammy cloth'. 'Mammy cloth' is a general term for real Dutch wax (also called Dumas after the man who first traded in it), imitation wax, real Java, imitation Java and fancy prints. This was followed by others: Ghana Textile Printing (GTP) in 1967 at Tema; Akosombo Textiles Limited (ATL) in 1968 at Akosombo. Japan used to export annually 764,000 square yards of printed cloth – 'African prints' – to Ghana; this figure dropped to 23,000 square yards in 1970 (*Japan Textile News*, no.198, May 1971) when cheaper, imported, imitation wax prints appeared on the market. Local factories were subsequently protected by a trade policy which banned the importation of textile prints. With today's free-market policy, 'mammy cloth' is now imported to Ghana from Holland, Britain, Nigeria, Togo, Ivory Coast and China. Ghanaian textiles are exported to the United States of America, Germany and Britain but are intended primarily for the local market; Ghanaian cloth has found its way to neighbouring markets and has occasionally been reimported.

Textile designs in Ghana are registered at the offices of the Registrar General's Department, Accra, for copyright protection and industrial property rights. The registry was established by an act of parliament in 1965 and so far has recorded about 3000 entries.

Young people (mostly men) with an aptitude for design are trained within the factory to acquire technical skills related to textile design. The work of designers in factories is usually to translate registered designs into positives for printing; factories seldom design and print their own cloth. They rarely employ College of Art graduates; however, vacation training has been offered in the factories to both male and female undergraduate textile designers. At GTMC, the current printing superintendent is a textile graduate from the College of Art, who was employed initially in the quality-control laboratory.

In the 1960s, some designers and artists submitted textile designs through agents to Ghana's new factories. One such designer was Grace Kwami, who sent three albums to Tema in the mid-1960s; nothing came of the venture though the designs were kept for over two years.

People involved in the naming of cloths comprise leading textile traders (mainly market women), the general public and local designers. Names are given to cloths by sellers in the market to boost sales; they are useful for identification and communication. Four out of five of all 'mammy cloths' have names; some merely describe motifs, for example, ABC, diamonds, peacock, scissors, etc.

The effect of wearing cloth with special meanings, ranging from the philosophical to the psychological, is still potent today. Some cloths commemorate events or celebrate heroes and beauties; others are proverbs embracing the folk wisdom of Ghana.

GTMC designer John Boham and self-employed designer Ben Lartey reported that commissions by individuals could start off with proverbs as working briefs. An example is the Akan proverb *owuo mpe bribe* ('death takes no bribe'), for which Lartey designed a motif of a skeleton whose arm reaches out but never touches a bundle of money. The printed cloth in indigo and white is intended as a funeral cloth for mourning those who die in old age in southern Ghana, a custom now observed by some Asante. Ben Lartey is a self-taught artist who gained experience at Patterson Zochonis & Sons Ltd and, lately, another textile distributing company, S.D. Karam & Sons Ltd, where he worked as chief designer with four assistants. These firms are no longer in the textile business but Lartey's reputation has extended to all the major textile-printing firms in Ghana.

Boham and Lartey design for specific manufacturing techniques. For a single pattern, there could be five variations in colour-blending, four to five colour combinations and twenty colour-ways from a range of ninety. Green, lemon-green, pink/green, yellow/purple/green, were cited as colours of the 1970s and 1980s. A lot of new colours are 'dirty', brownish, khaki, with bright colours blending for harmony and colour effect. With such a wide range of options available, colour is regarded as a secondary feature of design – secondary to structure, linear quality and shape. A recent trend on the Ghanaian fashion scene is a new fabric called *sheddar* (bazin or damask). The motifs in its weave enhance its look when it is over-printed; it therefore looks richer than ordinary wax prints from Holland. New fashions and fabrics inspire new designs.

Since 1972, the Technology Consultancy Centre of the University of Science and Technology, Kumasi, has been offering training and equipment for broadloom weavers. Looms are made at the College of Art, UST, after British prototypes. About ten weavers are trained over a two-year period. The mass production of *kente* broadloom weaves started in the 1980s, along with the intro-duction of lurex yarns, at Spintex Ltd. Lurex is now manufactured locally, in addition to imports from Japan, to meet a growing demand.

Julia Hilger

THE KANGA: AN EXAMPLE
OF EAST AFRICAN TEXTILE DESIGN

For the past 140 years the *kanga* has been one of the most popular garments on the East African coast. This rectangular cloth (110 x 150 cm), which is usually sold and worn in matching pairs, emerged during the 1850s from the islands of either Mombasa, Pate, Lamu or Zanzibar, influenced by the many different trading societies which had established themselves on the coast since the thirteenth century. Asian Muslims from the area of Kutch, India, for example, brought their multicoloured cloth, while Portuguese traders brought cotton handkerchiefs, which, if sewn together, make the rectangular shape of the *kanga*. These handkerchiefs are called *leso*, a name which is still used on the coast for a pair of *kanga*.

Originally, wooden printing blocks similar to those used in India were employed to create patterns on this cotton cloth. However, due to the large demand for *kanga*, foreign manufacturers, particularly companies in Britain, the Netherlands, India and (after 1945) also Japan and China, started to produce large quantities of screen-printed cloth for export to East Africa (by 1904, 1,559,439 kilograms of cotton cloth were imported into German East Africa alone). Due to this development, wooden printing blocks have not been used in East Africa since about 1910, and can now only be found in museums.

It was not until the late 1960s or early 1970s that locally manufactured *kanga* largely replaced those foreign imports, when Tanzania and Kenya were able to build integrated mills, the largest of which is Rivatex (Rift Valley Textiles) in Eldoret, Kenya. This mill currently produces up to 400,000 metres of *kanga* per month using a rotary print system, ensuring good quality and colouring. Their main competitors today are the Indian silk-screen printed cloths; a method which cannot guarantee the same print quality as rotary print. Despite the fact that many of these imports are of a lower quality, they are cheaper and therefore more affordable for many people in East Africa.

The name *kanga* derives from the Kiswahili word for the guinea fowl, a black-and-white speckled bird, which constantly chatters. According to the oral history, Waswahili men named this cloth, which is particular to women, after the bird, since the early designs featured small dots and flowers in black, white and red. More importantly, they thought that women chattered like the guinea fowl. Women, however, treasure their *kanga*. They are often given as gifts (in some regions the husband has to buy his wife four *kanga* every four months) and are usually kept in chests, some of them only to be worn on special occasions. Women might go out together wearing the same *kanga* in order to signal their friendship and *kanga* have also been used as a currency. At times of financial crisis they may be pawned by the women, but only by women, since although *kanga* are paid for by men they constitute part of a woman's wealth.

The *kanga* design is symmetrical; the artist designs one-half or one-quarter of the cloth on a piece of paper, which is then given to a printer to copy. It has four borders which are known as 'pindo' (hem) and the central area is known as 'miji' (town). Below the central motif, a motto or proverb is printed along one border. This proverb is thought to have been added in the early twentieth century by H.E. Abdullah Kaderdina, one of the oldest traders of cloth in Mombasa. His family, however, credits the

Paje, Zanzibar, 1994

addition, which gave the *kanga* its unique combination of image and text, to the creativity of Zanzibari women, who used the proverbs as a form of communication. Until the 1930s these mottos were printed in the Kiswahili language in Arabic script. It was then changed to Roman script in order to make it accessible to the non-Muslim market of Kiswahili speakers. Today one can also find inscriptions in English, which are aimed at the tourist market.

🕊 One of the earliest known designs is the *kitsutu* (p.107), probably named after a town in Tanzania. This particular *kanga* is given to young brides as part of their dowry, to cast off evil. Due to its ritual function, *kitsutu* do not always include a proverb. However, traders and manufacturers agree that in other cases the proverb is vital to the selling potential of *kanga*. Women choose their *kanga* according to three criteria: the proverb; the quality of the cloth and the printing; and finally, the design. Although there are no specific constraints upon the type of image to be used in the central area of the *kanga*, certain 'classic' designs are favoured and therefore reappear on the market, sometimes featuring different proverbs. One of these 'classic' patterns is the cashew nut (paisley-shaped pattern), which is a cash crop on the East African coast and therefore associated with wealth (p.109). In general, although the designs might be fairly abstract, to be successful the images used must be recognisable as part of the local environment.

🕊 Most *kanga* are designed by men, either by traders themselves, such as Abdullah Kaderdina, or at the design department of the mills such as Rivatex. There is one important exception: the late Fatma Shaaban Abdullah, an artist from Zanzibar who not only researched the cultural and historical roots of the *kanga*, but also created her own designs. Many of these were commissioned by political parties such as ASP (Afro-Shirazi Party) in Zanzibar, in order to commemorate a special occasion of either religious or political nature. One of her designs with the words, 'Hurrah to the car of the president' is illustrated on page 109. Not only did Fatma Abdullah exploit the communicative value of the *kanga*, she also tried to illustrate the relationship between text and image. In the case of the 'car', the motif clearly reflects the motto, but generally the patterns should be seen as a form of visual entertainment emphasising social, religious or political issues. Fatma Abdullah's *kanga* are innovative and popular due to her carefully chosen phrases and intricate designs. However, most women are less concerned to know who designed their *kanga*, and more interested in the phrases used and the overall pattern. Many of the designs have been given nicknames by women: for example, '*Maziwa ya mama ni tamu*' ('Mothers' milk is sweet') would be called 'cashew' because of the pattern on the border, or 'breast', due to the large circle in the middle (p.109); '*Usitupe chakukamata ukatumai cha kutafuta*' ('A bird in the hand is worth two in the bush') is called 'Eggs' (p.108); and '*Tujitahidi Kulima Njaa isitufisidi*' ('Let's try to harvest so that hunger does not harm us/kill us') (p.108) is a commemorative *kanga* made for the harvest celebration every August. It would be called 'eyes' or 'leaves'.

🕊 *Kanga* can also feature health warnings, such as 'One cannot eat poison without experiencing bitterness' or 'A housefly is

terror', while others describe relationships between husband and wife: 'Roam as you please, to me you will return' or 'I love you but. . .', favoured by women since the beginning of the century. During the late 1950s and early 1960s some of these phrases were so explicit that the colonial authorities and women's groups in Kenya attempted to ban them. (It should be borne in mind that at the time *kanga* were manufactured abroad, so the manufacturer would most probably not be able to understand the dual meanings of the proverbs.)

🕊 The Kenyan and Tanzanian governments and organisations such as the UN have recognised the propaganda value of *kanga* and use them as a channel of communication and for education. For example, in 1985 Rivatex were commissioned to make a design for the UN Decade for Women Conference, and the President of Kenya, Daniel arap Moi, had *kanga* designed as tablecloths for his official residence, promoting peace and unity, while in Tanzania many *kanga* emphasise the importance of mass education.

🕊 There is, however, a new threat to the future of the *kanga*. Since the 1980s second-hand clothes have been imported from Europe which compete with the cloth, as they are affordable and satisfy women's desire to be up-to-date. For the *kanga* to be entirely replaced by 'Western-style' clothes would be tragic, since with its disappearance, East Africa would not only lose an important means of communication, it would also lose a truly extraordinary artistic tradition.

Paje, Zanzibar, 1994

Simon Peers

WEAVING IN MADAGASCAR

Unlike much of East Africa, handloom weaving in the highlands of Madagascar is still a living, if not thriving, tradition. Since the sixteenth century, traders and travellers have commented on this indigenous weaving and have also been an important influence on the evolution of the textiles providing raw materials, dyes and certain designs. Ironically, these traders have also contributed to their decline by introducing cheap foreign/imported goods.

The *lamba* is the quintessential Malagasy cloth. The generic word *lamba* is used throughout the country to denote the rectangular cloth worn in a variety of ways according to the ethnic group or the specific ceremonial occasion attended. The textiles to be found today on the coast are generally printed machine-made cotton cloths, but particularly in the highlands and the south of the country, hand-woven textiles are still made and worn. An impressive variety of materials were used in the past to make different *lamba*, including fibres from plantain, the bark of various trees and spider's silk. Today raffia and bast are still being used along with more conventional and synthetic fibres.

As in so many cultures the most coveted material has always been, and still is, silk. In the highlands of the country among Betsileo and Merina peoples there are two main kinds of silk still used, resulting in two very different products. The indigenous silk comes from a variety of endemic silkworm. This is difficult to degum and results in a grey or brown spun silk with no shine or brilliance. It is used almost exclusively for the weaving of shrouds, or *lambamena*, which are prized for their durability and are consequently perfectly adapted to their role. Since funerary rites are still integral to Malagasy culture of the highlands the *lambamena* remains the best known of all handloom weaving in the country. However, the cost of these shrouds, often made up of eight woven panels sewn together, has meant that these textiles are now only accessible to the wealthy.

The second type of silk comes from the *Bombyx mori*, or Chinése silkworm, which is raised in the highlands, reeled and made into plain or patterned shawls, the latter known as *lamba akotofahana*. These textiles are generally undyed. Both kinds of textile are woven on the simplest fixed heddle and continuous warp looms, whose design has not changed for centuries. Such a brief description of the present state of silk weaving of the Merina in the highlands of Madagascar, however, belies a richer and more beautiful past, which deserves to be better known. Until the arrival of the British in the early nineteenth century, the Malagasy had woven their handsome *lamba* with Chinese silk that was imported by Arab and Indian traders. It was an Anglo-Irishman James Hastie who first introduced the mulberry tree to Madagascar and presented the first reeling machine to King Radama I.

Towards the end of the nineteenth century, European visitors to the country were already aware of the disappearance of a number of traditional arts and crafts. By the time the French colonised Madagascar in 1895 many traditions had been lost forever. Among these was the elaborately patterned and coloured silk weaving reserved for the royalty and wealthy class. These textiles were worn for special ceremonial occasions, such as the ceremony of circumcision or at funerals. On the death of one of these nobles the *lamba* also served as an outer covering for the shrouds, and were often placed in the tomb next to the body and beside other prized possessions. At that time there were two principal types of silk cloth with elaborate patterns and motifs, one known as the *valoharaka* and the other the *akotofahana*. Today the term *akotofahana* is the accepted generic term for all weaving with supplementary floating weft patterns, but now the traditional idiosyncratic motifs and bright colours are extinct. Even in the 1890s visitors were writing of the difficulty in finding these wonderful textiles. A combination of factors signalled the demise of the rich *lamba akotofahana*. In the 1860s, with the opening up of the country to foreign trade, imported textiles became very popular. In addition, the textiles were expensive and very time consuming for the Malagasy to produce. Today the women in the highlands who still wear the *lamba* drape their shoulders with a white cloth decorated with European designs, a distant cousin of the early nineteenth-century royal *lamba*.

Most commentators in the nineteenth century described the patterns appearing on these silk *lamba* as deriving from flowers and leaves and this may possibly link to the complicated system of honours. The word honour in Malagasy literally means those who are the flower of grass. Others have attributed a deeper meaning, finding in these designs the tree of life guarded by birds. There is in fact a surprising lack of detailed oral or written tradition concerning the making and significance of these cloths, but the *lamba* in its many forms was and still is an indication of rank in society. A better quality silk or workmanship, a more intricate and elaborate pattern, a larger cloth, and a choice of colours, all indicated wealth and standing.

Most weaving in Madagascar is a domestic and familial activity. People generally work alone at home rather than in groups. However, certain women's groups and associations do exist making cotton and silk *lamba*, tablecloths and bed covers. A more recent initiative that I have been involved with has attempted to recreate the nineteenth-century patterned, coloured textiles. The first attempt to revive the tradition was with a group of weavers in the southern highlands, but for numerous reasons this failed. It was soon followed by another attempt closer to the capital, at Arivonimamo, a town reputed for its weaving history and connections. Here I was fortunate in linking up with an immensely talented family of weavers who were young and keen to try something far more complicated than they were used to. The organisation began on a very small scale in the family house and gradually expanded, building larger versions of the traditional Malagasy loom and pedal looms to give greater flexibility and choice to width and length, while retaining the supplementary leashes that were used to make the warp and weft patterns.

🕮 Today there are ten weavers in the group who have formed themselves into an association, Valoharaka, which has given them a certain autonomy, while retaining a direct link with the small enterprise that we have founded, Lamba Sarl. A little

different from a mission artisan's description of the weavers in 1826 as they 'sit upon their heels weaving from morning to night a month for one-eighth of a Spanish Dollar'. One other revival of this type of weaving was attempted during the 1920s and 1930s when Madagascar was a French colony. This was instigated by a Frenchman, Pierre Heidmann, whose aim was primarily to display these textiles in the various colonial exhibitions.

🕮 Today this most demanding and intensive work has found its way into a number of museum collections. While reviving and reinventing tradition, this initiative has also focused attention on one of the most beautiful aspects of Madagascar's material culture.

Silk *lamba*
Mpanjaka Fotsy design
Madagascar, *c*.1995
(detail)
Collection Lamba Sarl

Boy's blanket (*ixakatho*)
Xhosa, Fingo, Eastern Cape, South Africa, acquired 1989
Standard Bank Collection
University of the Witwatersrand, Johannesburg

Rayda Becker

CLOTHING AND IDENTITY IN
SOUTHERN AFRICA

✋ The textiles from Southern Africa that are included in the exhibition, like many others from the African continent, are garments. Having once been worn, they are imbued, on one level, with 'human experience'.[1] On another level, they are complex objects linked to social passages within the communities from which they come and to the economic and political histories of the region. They are also a record of the unnamed women who made and wore them. Their presentation here as flat objects enables a reading of these garments as design formats, a place for pictorial distribution; yet that denies a vital part of their reality. In context, outside of a gallery or museum, they would be shaped, given form, and so completed by the body.

✋ None of these cloths were woven on hand-operated looms and so, strictly speaking, might not be considered textiles.[2] These materials are not part of the tradition of cotton weaving in the south-eastern region of the African continent, recorded as dating from the fifteenth century, and which was supplanted in the early twentieth century by factory-produced fabrics imported from India and Europe.[3] Each cloth exhibited is machine-made but has been enhanced with hand-worked additions. It is in these embellishments, as much as in the selection of the basic materials, that local and regional styles can be identified. Blankets, for example, are worn by both Ndebele in the Transvaal and Xhosa in the eastern Cape, but while the Ndebele select what is called a 'Middleburg' blanket with broad red, blue, yellow and brown stripes extending from a central green band,[4] in the eastern Cape, the Xhosa preference has always been for plain white (or occasionally red) blankets with a black stripe on either end. Many white blankets are then dyed with ochre (p.114).

✋ The reasons for such preferences are not always evident, although some explanations are offered by recent research; reasons which appear to depend as much upon historical as cultural factors and which therefore raise issues around the role that clothing has played in the construction of identity. The characteristic beadwork of Ndebele people, for example, emerged late in the nineteenth century after their defeat in

Married woman's apron (liphotho)
Vinyl, plastic, braid, rick-rack and other ready-made fabrics
Ndebele, Central Transvaal, South Africa, acquired 1985
Standard Bank Collection
University of Witwatersrand, Johannesburg

the Mapoch Wars. With the resulting dispersal of the Ndebele, clothing, in the form of beaded garments, became significant as markers of culture and identity within the diaspora of the Transvaal. Parallel stories of contemporary relevance are found in other dress forms. The decorative *minceka*, for example, which are usually made by Tsonga-speaking women, have provided a distinctive, visible sign of identity for women from the ex-'homeland' of Gazankulu in the north-eastern Transvaal; a style which has been adopted by some of their neighbours (*eg* Lobedu). Each cloth in the exhibition can be seen in such terms and may be related to the construction of identity; even the beaded back apron, the *sikomoka* from Zimbabwe (p.113). Made by the Tonga, who live on the shores of Lake Kariba, it is like no other local design and is characterised by the predominance of red, white and blue beads set out on dark cloth in horizontal registers of flattened triangles. Still other forms, such as the Xhosa blanket *ixakatho*, are recognised as representing a continuity with the past; a heritage recorded in paintings made by European colonial artists during the nineteenth century.

🌻 Questions of tradition and authenticity, indeed, inevitably arise when considering the textiles of Southern Africa. Certainly, if either is thought to rest upon the use of indigenous materials, then the place of these textiles is debatable given that all the fabrics were initially imported. The same applies to the glass beads, the use of which is now considered a 'tradition' of the region. South Africa, for all its industrialisation, does not manufacture glass beads, and so the inclusion of every glass bead involves far more than the choice of colour; it provides a record of exchange and trade.

🌻 Perhaps the best known of South African forms of design are Ndebele beadwork and mural painting, popularised through publications and the proximity of the makers to Pretoria. In the beadwork two main colour ranges are employed which, together with the size of the beads, can be used to date the pieces on which they are sewn. Earlier examples are characterised by the dominant use of white and in later pieces by blues, greens and black. The two *liphotho* (aprons) included in the exhibition (one is illustrated on p.49) probably date to the 1960s. Both are adaptations of earlier aprons which were made of hide and, importantly, retain the shape of the older, 'traditional' rectangular form with square panels and a central fringe along the lower edge. The persistence of this design is accounted for by the fact that it is shape, rather than colour or the minor design elements, that carries the code which identifies the wearer as Ndebele, female and married. As an outward sign, then, of the status of the woman, the lower edge may be interpreted further:

the two panels as representing the partners in the marriage, and the tassled, beaded fringe indicating the children they might produce.

🌻 The supports of both aprons are ready-made materials: canvas and vinyl, the latter being an interesting, though short-lived variant. 'Plastici' is the name given by Ndebele women to all those items made from plastics and synthetic materials[5] which can be rationalised in a number of ways: as the art of the poor, or according to style or regional variations. Braided vinyl aprons are, however, no longer made, since the commercial market, into which so much of Ndebele art now feeds, wants beads. Authenticity is contained, it seems, in beads rather than braid. Such *liphotho* are worn together with a back skirt, beaded arm and leg rings and beaded neck hoops: rings of metal or their plastic imitations. A blanket *irari* (other vernacular names exist for the blanket) is usually worn to cover the torso and it is here that some of the most elaborate beadwork from the region can be found. Generally made in separate strips, the beadwork is subsequently attached to the blanket in horizontal bands. Over the years the imagery has changed from a more minimal use of abstract forms and now includes more recognisable images, which reflect a response to the modern world. There are pitched-roof houses, electric lights, lettering and the '*ufly*' (aeroplanes).

🌻 The same matching of industry and identity informs the *minceka* (the plural form of *nceka*) made by women in the northern Transvaal. Two are usually worn, one tied across each shoulder covering the torso and a large underskirt. These are public, non-ritual garments and all kinds of intervention and innovation have occurred around and on them. Traders and local women have become involved in selecting colours and designs for the popular highly coloured printed *minceka*[6] and a wide range of manufactured items, from thread to safety pins, brass rings and plastic hair ornaments, have been included, turning some *minceka* into virtual collages. The image range is equally wide. Abstract, emblematic and figurative forms are combined with ease in one piece. At times the maker also names herself in large lettering, a nod in the directions of literacy, change, modernity.

🌻 The base fabrics used in Southern Africa are thus transformed.

1 🌻 See A.B.Weiner and J.Schneider, 1989
2 🌻 See John Picton and John Mack, 1989
3 🌻 See Patricia Davison and Patrick Harries, 1980
4 🌻 Named as Middleburg blankets after one of the larger towns in the central Transvaal where the Ndebele live, an accommodation of custom by commerce.
5 🌻 Ivor Powell, 1995
6 🌻 Bronwen Findlay, 1995

Jackie Guille

SOUTHERN AFRICAN TEXTILES TODAY:
DESIGN, INDUSTRY AND COLLECTIVE ENTERPRISE

In any review of the textiles produced in Southern Africa, it is necessary to consider the socio-cultural and economic conditions of the region. The phase-down of protective tariffs for the clothing and textile industry is a key issue in the current economic debate in South Africa, while the textile industry in Zimbabwe and Zambia, lacking the capital to invest in new plant, has retrenched, resulting in widespread job losses. In recent years climatic changes in the region have brought successive droughts, reducing, if not all but destroying, the cotton crop, increasing the cotton lint price and production costs. But the most significant problem afflicting all of sub-Saharan Africa is the flooding of the local markets with imported second-hand clothing. These clothes are of good quality, often having little wear, and sell at a price which undercuts locally produced textiles.

In Zaire in the mid-1970s, there was a revival in the demand for 'African' prints following the re-election in 1970 of President Mobutu, who began a gradual process of de-Westernisation by decree. Western names were exchanged for African ones and towns such as Leopoldville (now Kinshasa) were renamed. Western dress was forbidden and *chitenge* cloth, printed in distinctive 'African' patterns, was much sought after and once again became the norm.[1] Commemorative fabrics, celebrating a variety of political or religious groups, also enjoyed widespread popularity throughout Southern Africa and frequently incorporated photographic portraits of prominent figures.

Chitenge cloth, like the plaid patterned *kikoy* and boldly printed *kangas* of East Africa, is sold in two-metre lengths which are worn wrapped around the waist and falling to the ankles, although it is also made up into shirts and dresses.[2] The imagery displays symbolic and simple geometric motifs, repetitive designs and textural patterns, representations of human beings, animals, mythical figures and masks. Elements are taken both from existing fabrics and from graphic arts such as advertising and packaging, reflecting urban life.

In the early 1970s, factories were established in Zaire and also in adjacent Zambia. Setting up printworks in Africa was a difficult undertaking as a start had to be made with several hundred workers who had no experience of textile printing, never having seen a machine or even the inside of a factory. Sotexki in Kisangani, run by Maurer Textiles (Switzerland), began *chitenge* production in 1974, employing rotary screen and hand-block printing in a variety of techniques to produce 'African', Java, resist and reserve, and real wax prints. Sotexki continues to produce original designs but production has been drastically reduced with the prevailing political uncertainty in Zaire. The company's design archive, embracing the total history of their production, documents the unique position of 'African' design in the production of textiles and their influence on the cultural identity of the region.

The production in Zambia, Malawi and Zimbabwe is of the easier imitation wax prints, 'Imiwax' – direct prints made to look like wax resists with mock cracking – and 'fancies' – strikingly coloured, patterned prints. Zambia gained independence in 1964 and was governed by a 'One-party Participatory Democracy' headed by Kenneth Kaunda until a new constitution permitting a Multi-Party Democracy was introduced in 1991. In the October 1991 elections the Movement for Multi-Party Democracy (MDD) swept the polls and its leader Frederick Chiluba became President of the Third Republic. Following these elections, there was a lifting of trade restrictions, and manufactured products from all over the region and overseas are now freely available in Zambia.

Cheap fabrics, copies of 'African' designs, produced in the Far East have flooded the market, supplanting the local textile products. Designs from Zaire and West Africa are plagiarised by Chinese, Japanese, Indian and Pakistani manufacturers who are able to access the latest technology, increasing productivity while reducing costs. It is not uncommon for a new design produced by Sotexki to be copied to the last detail in the Far East, with even the company name reappearing on the selvedge, and exported back to the African market. In the local market, sales of *chitenge* fabrics are determined by price and the popularity of the design rather than the quality of the cloth.

With the 'liberalisation' of trade, sales of locally produced *chitenge* fabric have slumped, forcing companies to close or restructure, rationalising their operation. Companies have shed over half their work force, but further savings are unlikely to be made in this area. For example, a weaver at Mulungushi Textiles Ltd earns only 20,000 kwacha (£17) per month – half the minimum wage – but the company would simply not survive if the wage bill were doubled. Production of *chitenge* fabrics is dwindling, the industry having turned its attention away from the expensive processes of dyeing and printing, and towards the securing of export markets for their 'grey' cloth and undyed yarn.

Kafue Textiles of Zambia Ltd (KTZ) is a parastatal company which Maurer Textiles, who hold 22 per cent of the shares, operate in tandem with their sister company Sotexki in Zaire. The factory at Kafue, 40 kilometres south of Lusaka, is equipped for rotary screen printing and officially opened in March 1970.

Most of the studio designers are self-taught beyond secondary school but George Muchinda, Head of Design, was sent to the UK in 1977 to train for a year within the Tootal group and then in Geneva. Today, however, none of the designers are exposed to even the local or regional market and the number employed has shrunk from twelve to four, who now devote their skills to

Designs for factory-printed cloth
Kafue Textiles, Zambia
Gouache on paper, c.1990

copying 'proven' designs. The local traders commission the company to reproduce popular fabrics, produced by other companies in Zaire, Nigeria and Japan, which are known to have a ready market. The KTZ archive of 'original' painted designs and fabric swatches is infinitely livelier than these copies, but as profit margins have been slashed, the company cannot afford speculative production of new designs.

🕯 KTZ no longer produces commemorative fabrics, many of which depicted the former president Kenneth Kaunda, as these displays are associated with the previous discredited regime.

🕯 Mulungushi Textiles Ltd (MTZ), a parastatal company, was set up at Kabwe in the early 1970s, facilitated by loans and technical assistance from the Chinese Government and production started in 1982. The Chinese supplied the plant, equipping the factory for spinning and weaving together with an engraved copper roller printing system and provided technical assistance until 1993.

🕯 The engraved roller printing machine employs hollow cylinder(s), having a thick deposit of copper on a steel core, on which the pattern is engraved. The pattern is printed from colour held in the grooved surface of the copper and given up to the cloth by pressure. One advantage of this method is that the engraved copper cylinders are stronger and possibly longer lasting than the more fragile metal mesh of rotary screens.[3] The mechanical means of mill and pentagraph engraving used by MTZ dates back to the early nineteenth century.

🕯 The conventional roller printing machines used by MTZ can produce extremely fine and high quality prints, but to do so they require expert handling by skilled operatives with years of experience. The withdrawal of Chinese technical assistance has left a vacuum in the training and supervision of skilled engravers. Consequently, the production quality of the current fabrics is clearly deteriorating, as some of the craftsmanship is slipping away.

🕯 The two designers currently at MTZ both had art training beyond secondary school before joining the company in 1989. Unlike Kafue Textiles, MTZ continues to produce original designs and commemoratives by commission – recent examples have been done for the MDD elections depicting Chiluba and the ANC for the South African elections – together with copies of existing fabrics.

🕯 Zambia does not have as large a tourist trade as Zimbabwe or South Africa and has few outlets for local crafts. Very simple batik and tie-dyed fabrics are produced, the technique having been introduced by expatriate Ghanaian and Nigerian wives. The weaving, initiated and supported by Danish volunteers, displays the Scandinavian influence in its simple bands of pastel-coloured plain weave. There is no extant tradition in Zambia but in pre-colonial days 'plain white' cloth was traditionally woven in the Eastern Province.

🕯 The spinning and weaving of cotton cloth was already being practised in Zimbabwe in the thirteenth century and possibly earlier than that. Because the climate on the high veld plateau was cool, clothing was necessary and the Shona had developed an excellent but somewhat laborious spinning and weaving technique. Archaeological excavations at the site of Great Zimbabwe have revealed hundreds of discs cut from potsherds that were used as spinning weights – the only remains of a once flourishing textile industry.

🕯 Cloth was imported to Zimbabwe from India, cotton cultivation and weaving (the production of *machira*, cotton cloth woven on low wooden ground looms) being introduced by the Muslim traders at the same time. There is no evidence that this weaving is practised today. The present textile industry in Zimbabwe was set up in the early 1950s to meet local demand and quickly established a manufacturing base producing 'fancy' prints for the settler population and for export to Europe.

🕯 Today, many of the problems afflicting the Zambian industry are echoed in Zimbabwe. Undercut by second-hand clothing, Cone Textiles, the largest employer in the industry, went into liquidation in January 1995 and David Whitehead Ltd, founded at Hartley (Chegutu) in 1951, is struggling to survive.

🕯 David Whitehead employs rotary screen printing, producing 'European' styles, commemoratives and Java prints. All of the designers in the company's Harare studio were trained at Bulawayo Polytechnic, the only formal programme in commercial textile design available in Zimbabwe, which perpetuates conservative, Eurocentric tastes.

🕯 There are examples of successful enterprises – Deadly Dezign Ltd employs the talents of local artists to produce hand-printed T-shirts, floormats and paper products, for both the local and overseas markets.

🕯 Economic development has been the catalyst for increased activity in the crafts and the provision of training programmes in textiles and other crafts is largely undertaken by non-governmental organisations and craft cooperatives, particularly those involving women's groups both in the townships and the rural areas. Many are funded and facilitated by the International Aid agencies, priority being given to imparting practical skills to enable income generation. Craftspeople in many areas rely on the natural environment as the source of their materials and the increase in craft products, primarily sold to the tourist, raises serious environmental issues. These craft products are variable in quality but there are examples of both skill and invention, embracing tradition not as a static entity but as an ongoing and developing process.

🕯 The story of Weya Art, an offshoot from the Weya Community

Training Centre, situated in the centre of Weya Communal Area 170 kilometres from Harare, illustrates the dilemmas that confront even the most celebrated ventures.[4]

🜲 At the end of 1987, Ilse Noy came to Weya seeking to develop courses based on traditional crafts, but the only crafts actively practised by the women were knitting and crocheting, products which were not considered 'African' enough for the Western market and having a limited local market. Early in 1987, the centre replaced the unsuccessful machine sewing course with training in hand sewing, as individual dressmakers could not compete with the market prices offered by a well-established clothing industry.

🜲 Building on their sewing skills, Ilse began training the women in appliqué, embroidery and later in drawing and painting. The craft works produced benefited from her commitment and guidance. The original intent was income generation but also produced a considerable artistic development within the community. The works are an expression of the traditions and present-day life of the women artists.

🜲 At first this may sound like a story of pure success, the women having gained economic independence and self-confidence, their considerable monthly income far exceeding the income of most of their husbands, fathers and brothers. But the Weya artists, especially the young unmarried women, were seen by 'ordinary' villagers as a threat to the existing hierarchy of the community. At the same time the young women were attracted to life in the town, with its promise of freedom from family restrictions and village control. As a consequence, some of these women left Weya to work individually and collectively in Harare and 'side marketing' has increased, reducing the income feeding back to the centre and threatening quality control. Consequently 'Weya' style art is found in all manner of craft and curio shops and public markets.

🜲 One of Zimbabwe's most successful cooperatives, Cold Comfort Farm outside Harare, opened the Amon Shonge Gallery in May 1991. The gallery was established as a sales outlet for the art of women, mainly from rural backgrounds. The gallery provides an inviting exhibition space and further assists through technical and practical training. The gallery markets the works, among others, of Cold Comfort Weaving, Weya Art and Fambidzanai. The latter produce screen-printed fabrics, mostly single primary colours overprinted onto a brightly coloured tie-dyed background.

🜲 Ilse Noy has also played a significant role in the development of the Cold Comfort Farm Weaving workshop, which opened in 1985. At that time, six women were producing tapestries : today, the number has grown to around twenty. Initially the production was almost entirely self-sufficient – using locally available plants and roots to dye the raw wool. Having established a market for the woollen tapestries, the income generated provided monies to invest in cotton yarns and synthetic dyestuffs. Smaller, finely detailed cotton works, employing brightly coloured and more personalised images,were produced but these tapestries were priced beyond their market. The tapestry workshops have since reverted to copying old works and the use of cotton yarn discarded.

🜲 The various problems confronting many projects are complex,

Faith Chibanda, Christine Makoni and Nester Mufunde
Witch Craft
Panels of cotton with hand and machine applied appliqué,
padded relief elements and embroidery
Weya Communal Area, Zimbabwe, 1988
Collection Johannesburg Art Gallery

Left to right, top row : Funeral in village / Dead body is taken to graves / Witches taking the body from grave.
Second row : Sharing meat, cutting themselves pieces / Sharing unequal, start of fight; another cutting a hand / During fight the sun was rising; two others run away holding their pieces of meat.
Third row : The two found handcuffed at the grave / Dropped pieces put in a sack for reburial / Witches taken to Chief for judgement.
Bottom row : They are at the Chief's place waiting for their judgement / They were to pay one goat and a girl /Witches chased away.

having their origins in both the social structure of the community and the individual aspirations of the women. Furthermore, the role of the volunteer as facilitator often poses the question of what ultimate legacy they leave behind. Many ventures face stagnation or worse, total collapse, after their departure.

🜲 The interesting development that has taken place in the southern city of Bulawayo is the recent relocation of the City Art Gallery to the elegant colonial building of Douslin House, situated in the heart of the city centre. Behind the gallery, a number of artists' workshops are situated round the attractive open courtyard, offering both affordable work-space and opportunities for the artists to sell their works. Several are occupied by groups of women producing hand-painted and *sadza* (maize meal) fabrics.

South Africa also has a large and growing crafts industry based upon a wealth of traditional crafts and exemplified in the beadwork of the Zulu and Ndebele peoples. The Zulus originally made beadwork for ritual purposes. Later it was also made to satisfy the tourist demand for authentic curios but now it has been elevated into an artform. The 'new' beadwork depicts objects such as animals, planes and transistor radios together with tableaux showing scenes from daily life. The glass beads originally used in the sculptures were imported but plastic beads and items such as buttons, artificial flowers and plastic toys are now incorporated into the sculptures.

The African Arts Centre in Durban, established in the 1960s by the late Jo Thorpe, was initially a project of the Institute of Race Relations and became an autonomous project in 1984. Its guiding principle is to shift public opinion and artists' self perceptions away from the idea of tourist curios towards a focus on African art as an authentic aesthetic expression in its own right. It has played a pivotal role in establishing a market for emerging craft centres, particularly in Natal – KwaZulu.

The ELC Art and Craft Centre, or simply Rorke's Drift as it is best known, has been owned and managed by the Evangelical Lutheran Church in Southern Africa (ELCSA) since its beginning in the 1960s. The home of world-famous artists like the late John Muafangejo, the centre produces pottery, hand-printed fabrics, rugs and tapestries – the latter displaying bold patterns, based on Zulu designs, and figurative images of rural life.

The Dakawa Art and Craft Project in Grahamstown started as a Swedish International Development Aid (SIDA) funded textile printing workshop in the ANC's refugee camp in Dakawa in Tanzania. When the refugees were repatriated the workshop also 'moved home'. The project officially opened on 17 October 1992, with about twelve trainees in each workshop and it is committed to building on the art and craft tradition of South Africa, developing the use of new materials and modern techniques. Dakawa admits people only on the basis of their artistic ability, thus giving an opportunity to those who have not necessarily had a formal education. There are close links with Rorke's Drift – training is provided at Dakawa for crafts people who will return to the ELC Centre to pass on the expertise gained.

Hand-crafted textiles throughout Southern Africa employ similar techniques – woven tapestries, tie-dye, screen printed fabrics and *sadza* resist – but projects such as Pakhamani Textiles in Durban are breaking new ground in marketing their products in both the craft and commercial sectors.

Pakhamani (Zulu for 'to uplift myself') was founded by Gem Melville. The project comprises a group of women producing hand-painted cloths employing *sadza* resist. Generally, a base colour is painted over the whole fabric before the design is applied using a *sadza* porridge, which acts as a resist. The design is coloured by hand-painting textile pigment between the *sadza* outlines. When dry, the *sadza* is removed by scraping and washing, revealing the coloured outlines of the design. The fabrics display motifs and colours drawn from a wide range of sources – West African, Zulu and Ndebele wall painting, as well as European and Indian ceramic and textile motifs. Being hand painted, these fabrics are expensive, available only in galleries and fashionable stores, which limits their market and profitability.

Seeking to reach a wider market, Pakhamani have entered into a licensing agreement with one of the major textile companies, David Whitehead & Sons Ltd Natal. The company is producing a range of Pakhamani designs, to be marketed and promoted under the project's name. In reproducing these designs industrially, great care and attention has been given to the simulation of the brush strokes and idiosyncrasies which characterise the original craft products.

David Whitehead produces fashion and furnishing fabrics for the South African, Australian and American markets. Their printed collections continue to be dominated by classic floral patterns, which have a proven market, conservative and 'Eurocentric', for this is where the purchasing power lies. Their collaborative venture with Pakhamani is a new departure, promising not only to be a wise commercial decision but also to promote the company's support for the policy of affirmative action.

Looking towards the future, the South African textile industry faces many of the issues confronting the region as a whole. In Southern Africa, access to education and training and the role played by the international community in shaping educational agendas are burning issues. The matching of skills – acquired in the differing educational systems and cultural and physical environments – to previously held perceptions of visual norms and academic standards is part of the ongoing debate. The opportunity and undoubted challenge exist for the development of a fresh approach to textiles embracing and sustaining both traditional practice and contemporary culture.

1 Joyce Storey, 1978, pp.127-31
2 Judith von D.Miller, 1974, p.57
3 Joyce Storey, 1974, pp.68-104
4 Ilse Noy, 1992

Design for engraving for wax-print textile
Indonesian-derived design
'Mask', 'Back of Tortoise', or 'Chain'
Early 20th century
Collection A. Brunnschweiler & Co., Hyde

Fabric coffin (*niombo*)
Early 20th century

Niombo
Fabric coffin of imported blankets
Sundi-Kongo *c.*1938
Etnografiska Museet
Gothenburg, Sweden

Raffia textile
with cut-pile and cotton embroidery
Kuba, Zaire, early 20th century
Collection Peter Adler

Woven skirt
Raffia with appliqué and cut-pile embroidery
Kuba, Zaire, early 20th century
Collection Peter Adler

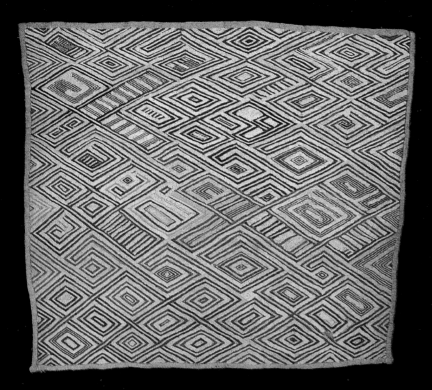

Woven skirt
Raffia with appliqué
Kuba, Zaire, 20th century
Collection Peter Adler

Sunset
Wool tapestry by Ashour Messelhi, Egypt, 1983
265 x 200 cm
Ramses Wissa Wassef Art Centre

Cotton appliqué
by Salah El Din M. El Ozy, 1995
Inscription : Say it to the one who knows it all
You might have learnt something, but many things
have slipped you by !
[Abu Nawas]

Hand-dyed cotton appliqué by Chant Avedissian
1989-90
Collection the artist

Man's gown
Cotton with silk embroidery
Ségou, Mali c.1880
Musée de l'Homme, Paris

Narrow-strip blanket
Machine-spun cotton
Mali, 1994
Private collection

Overleaf ☛
Narrow-strip cotton textile
Manjaka or Papel, Guinea Bissau, early 20th century
Trustees of the British Museum

65 | WEST AFRICA: MALI

Narrow-strip blanket by Oumar Bocoum
Machine-spun cotton
Mali, 1989
Collection Marine Biras

Overleaf ☛
Textile for wrap-around skirt
Cotton with viscose and lurex float-weave
with images of Pope Jean-Paul II
Senegal, *c.*1992
Private collection

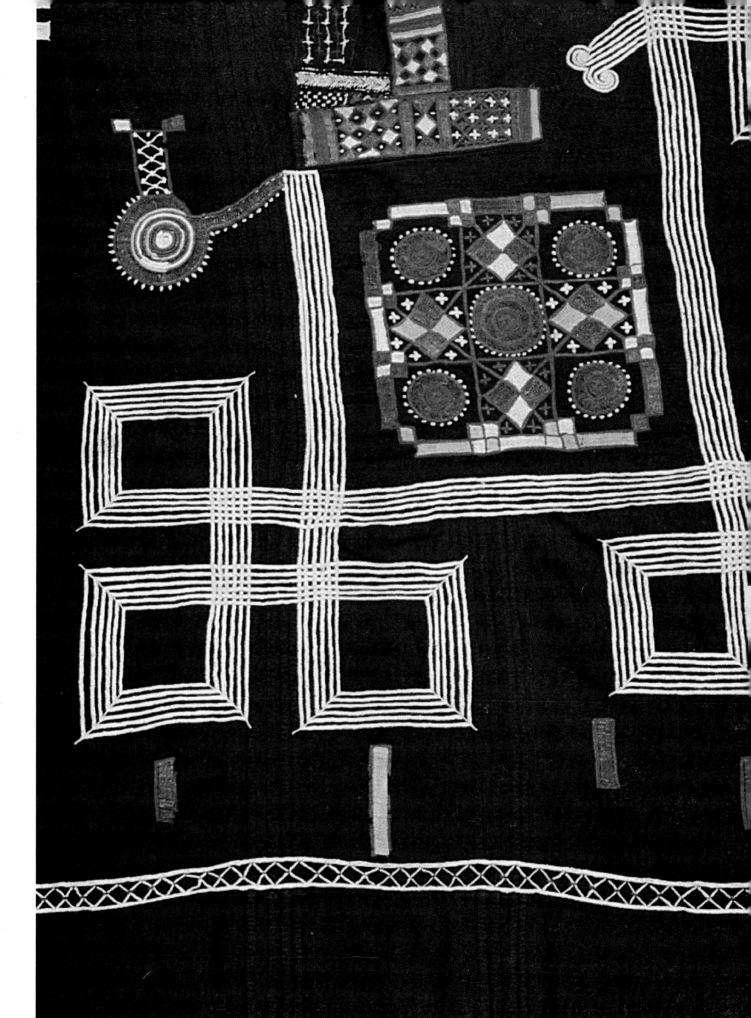

Page 67
Embroidered gown
Indigo-dyed cotton
Sierra Leone *c.*1920
Horniman Museum
London

Cotton textile
Tie-dyed in indigo and kola
Ivory Coast, 1970
Private collection

Tie-dyed viscose textile
Cloth purchased Liverpool,
dyed Sierra Leone *c.*1990
Collection Afrograph

Alidjau Tuiduille
wearing indigo tie-dyed
cotton gown
Ivory Coast 1973

Tie-dyed cotton damask
Kabala, Sierra Leone, acquired 1977
Horniman Museum
London

Cotton damask for gown tie-dyed by Gogo Semega Maiga
Bamako, Mali, 1994
Private collection

Tie-dyed cotton damask for gown
Bamako, Mali, 1994
Private collection

Undoing stitch-resist
Sewn in Mauritania, dyed in Mali
October 1994

Stitch resist-dyed cotton damask for gown
Bamako, Mali, 1994
Private collection

Tie-dyed cotton textile by Toyin Oguntona
Zaria, Nigeria, 1994
Private collection

Man's gown
Cotton with embroidery
Hausa (?), Nigeria, early 20th century
Collection Peter Adler

Overleaf (left) ☞
Man's gown
Shabka design (detail)
Factory-woven cotton
with wild silk embroidery
Hausa, Kano
Nigeria, *c*.1950
Private collection

Man's gown, *Yar Ilori* ('Daughter of Ilorin') design (detail of back)
Indigo-dyed hand-spun cotton with wild silk embroidery by Malam Suleiman
Hem lined with blue factory-woven cotton, Hausa, Zaria, Nigeria, 1973
Private collection

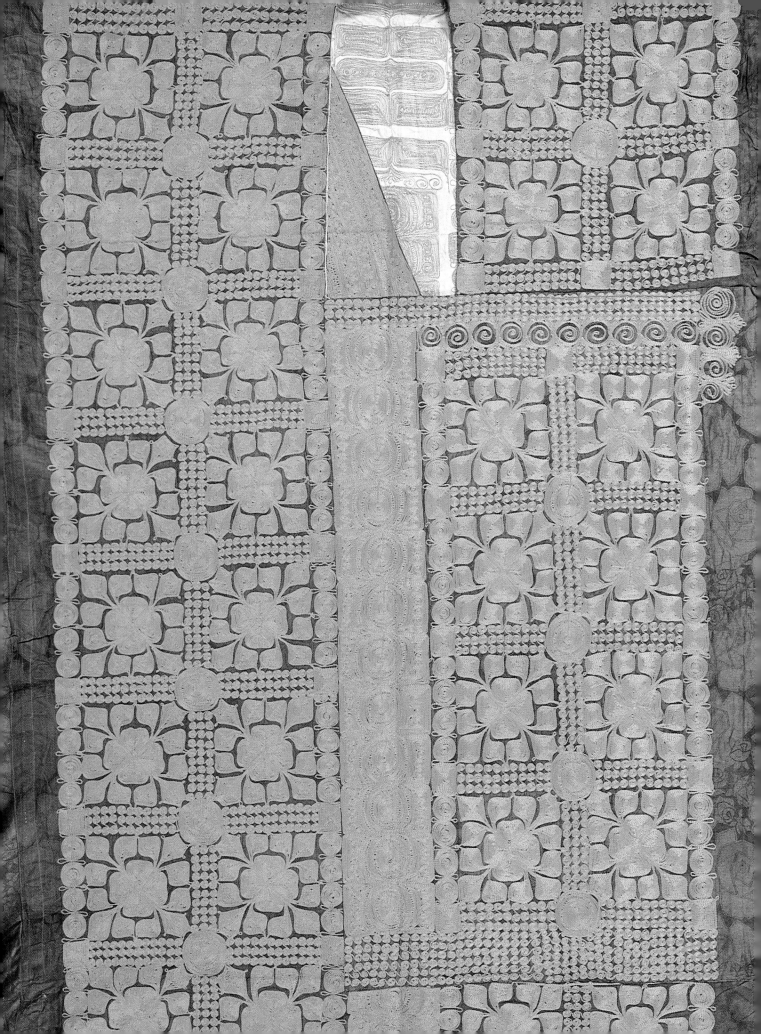

Man's gown
Yar Kumasi
('Daughter of Kumasi')
design
Machine embroidery
on cotton damask
Hausa, Zaria
Nigeria, 1975
Private collection

King's crown
Beads stitched to cotton
over basketry base
Yoruba, Nigeria,
20th century
Collection Peter Adler

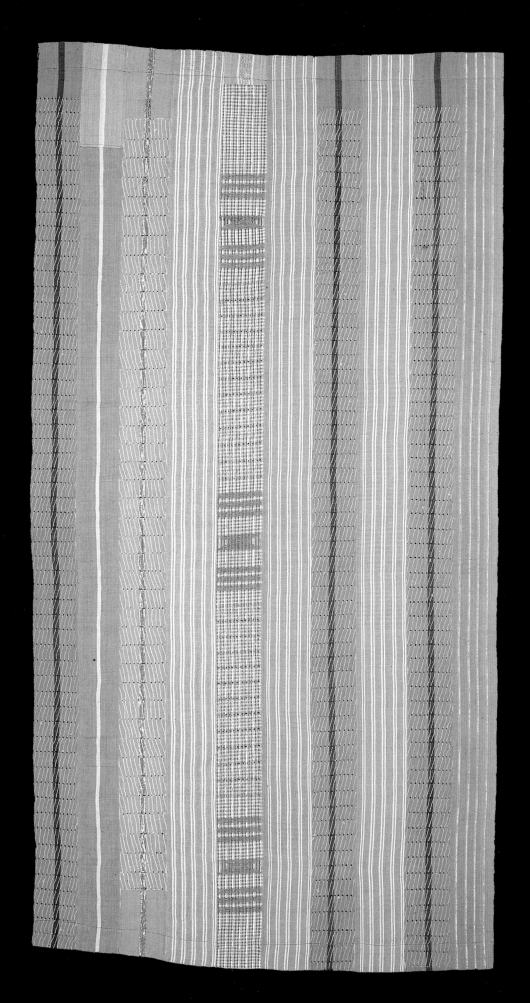

Narrow-strip textile
(*aso oke*)
Cotton and lurex
Yoruba, Nigeria, 1977
Trustees of the National Museums
of Scotland, Edinburgh

Narrow-strip textile (*aso oke*)
Cotton with supplementary weft-float design
Yoruba, Nigeria,
20th century
Collection Peter Adler

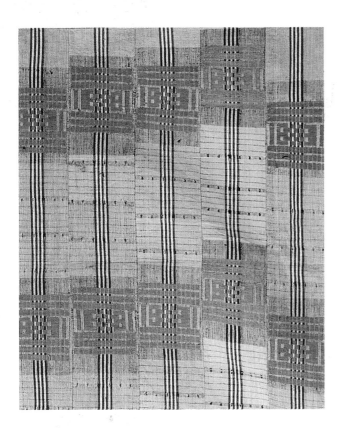

Narrow-strip textile (*aso oke*)
Cotton, rayon, and lurex
with supplementary weft-float design
Yoruba, Nigeria, 1977
Trustees of the National Museums
of Scotland, Edinburgh

Narrow-strip textile (*aso oke*)
Cotton with *ikat* stripes in the warp
Yoruba, Nigeria,
20th century
Collection Judith Appio

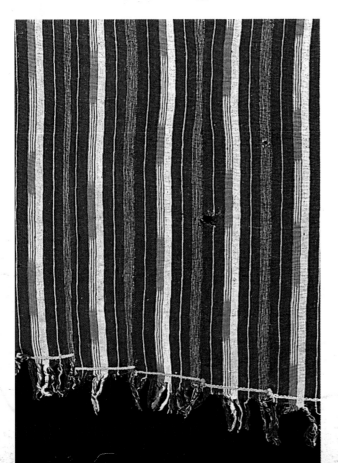

Narrow-strip textile (*aso oke*)
Cotton with openwork
Yoruba, Nigeria,
20th century
Collection Judith Appio

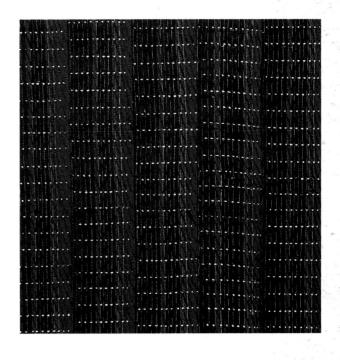

Indigo
resist-dyed
cotton
textile
(adire)
Yoruba
Nigeria
20th century
Collection
Judith Appic

Narrow-strip
cotton textile
(aso oke)
Yoruba
Nigeria
20th century
Collection
K.P., Paris

Indigo
starch resist-dyed
cotton textile
(*adire*)
with hand-painted
design
Yoruba, Nigeria,
20th century
Collection Judith Appio

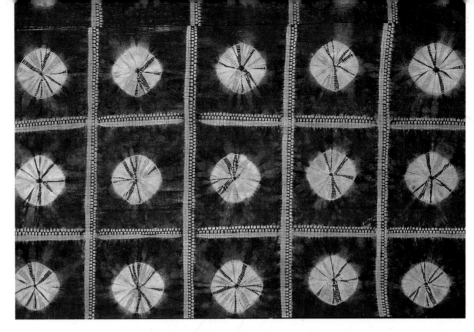

Indigo
resist-dyed
cotton
textile
(*adire*)
Yoruba
Nigeria
20th century
Collection
Judith Appio

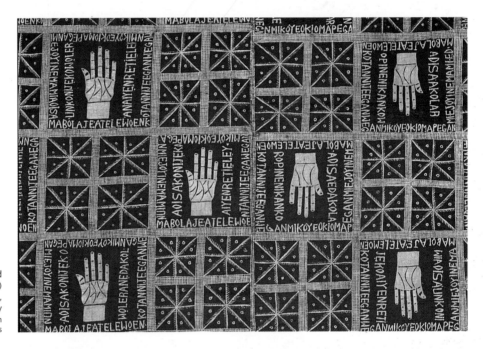

Indigo starch resist-dyed
cotton textile (*adire*)
Yoruba, Nigeria,
20th century
Collection
Alec and Helen Travers

Indigo stitch-resist
and tie-dyed
cotton textile (*adire*)
Yoruba, Nigeria,
20th century
Collection Judith Appio

My Village
Embroidery by Nike Olaniyi-Davies
*c.*1970
Collection the artist

Cotton textile
with knitting wool
Ijebu Ode
1930-45
Trustees of the National Museums
of Scotland, Edinburgh

Cotton textile
with rayon supplementary
weft-float design
Igbo, Akwete, Nigeria
1977
Trustees of the National Museums
of Scotland, Edinburgh

Cotton and viscose textile
woven on upright broadloom
in imitation of Ewe or Ewe-style narrow strip textiles
Igbo, Akwete, Nigeria, c.1937
Fowler Museum of Cultural History
University of California, Los Angeles

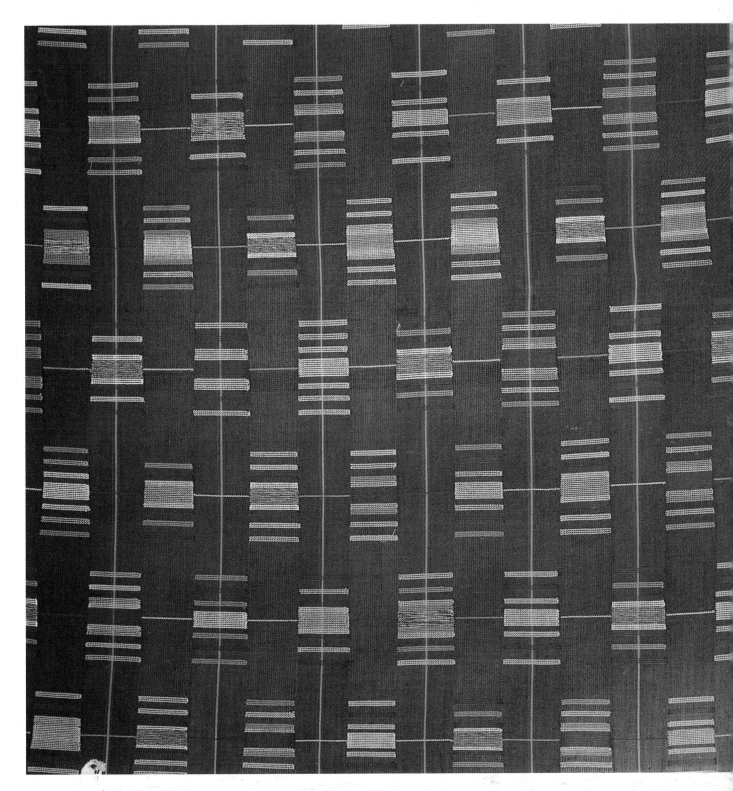

Overleaf ☛
Cotton textile, Igbo, Akwete, Nigeria, 20th century
Trustees of the British Museum

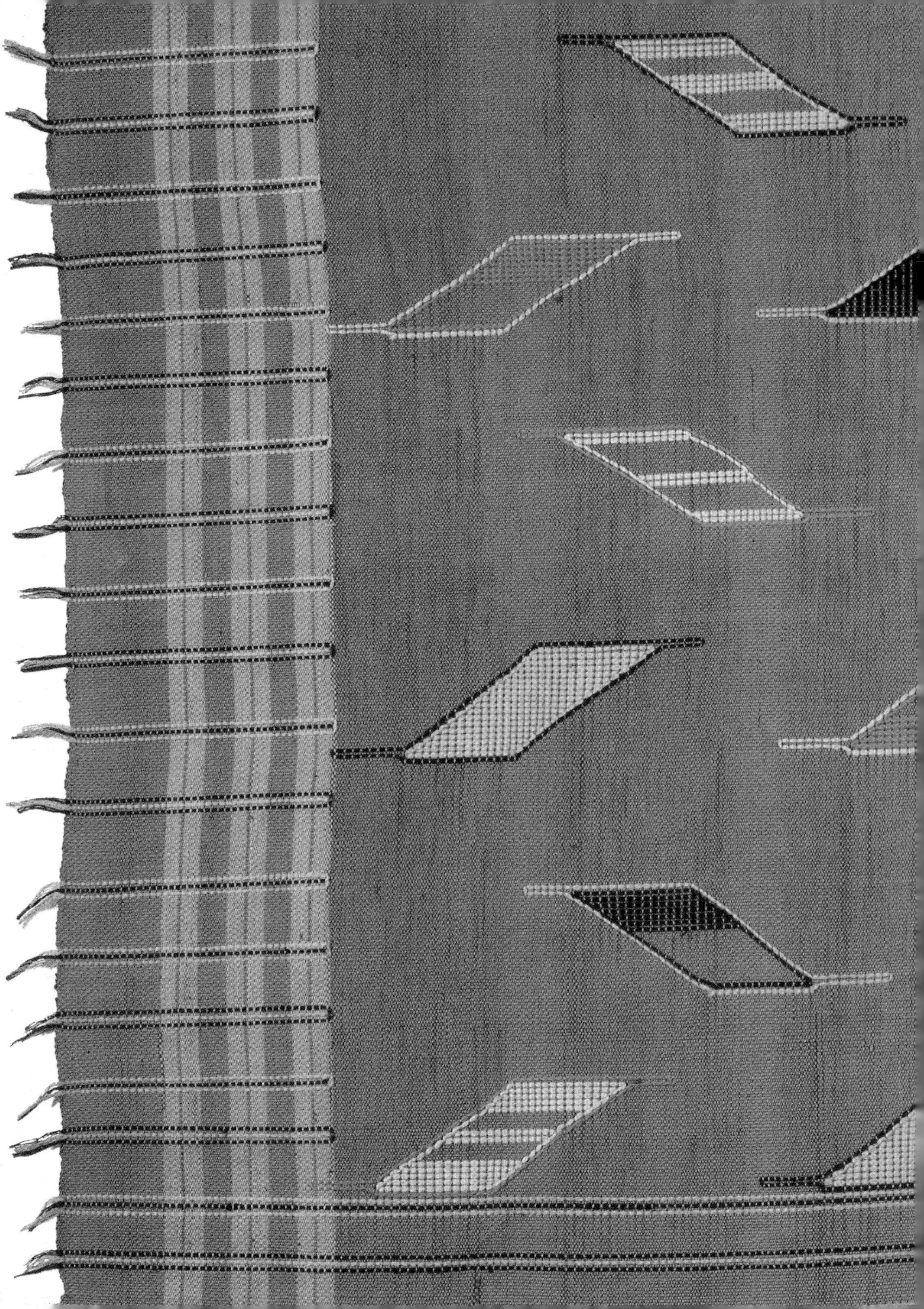

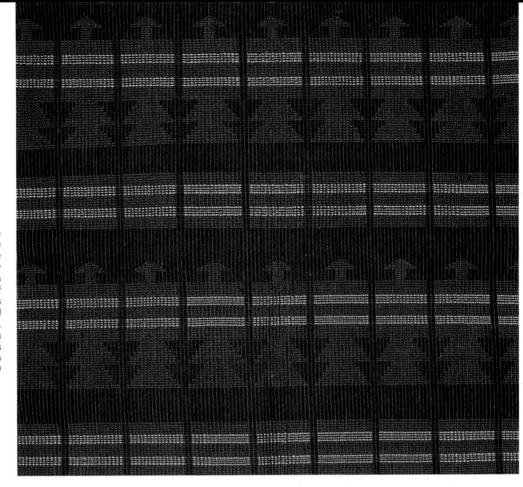

Cotton textile
with supplementary
weft motifs
Nupe, Nigeria
c.1930-40
Collection Peter Adler

Machine-spun
cotton textile
with viscose
supplementary
weft-float design
in shape of
Qur'an boards
Ebira, acquired
Okene market,
Nigeria
Late 1960s
Collection
John and Susan Picton

Cotton textile
with supplementary
weft-float design
Ebira, Nigeria
1976-7
Trustees of the
National Museums
of Scotland
Edinburgh

Factory-woven cotton cloth resist-dyed in indigo
North-eastern Igbo-speaking area, for Leopard Society of Ejagham,
Efik and other peoples of the Cross River region, Nigeria
20th century
Collection Judith Appio

Ngwomo
(memorial shrine)
with cloth by
Udoh Umor Aran Ekot
of Abiakpang,
Ikot Essien village
Seen at Mbiaso village, Anang
Mid-1970s

Okun Akpan Abuje
preparing to sew
patchwork panels
using a special
tensioning device
attached to his big toe
Mid-1970s

Factory-woven cotton appliqué and patchwork (detail)
by Okun Akpan Abuje, for memorial shrine to a deceased man
Ikot Obong, Afaha Clan, Ikot Ekpene, Anang, Nigeria, mid-1970s
Collection Keith Nicklin and Jill Salmons

Okakagbe dance troupe wearing costumes
by Lawrence Ajanaku, 1973
In the foreground, Ata Aosi in white, shakes the hand of Lawrence Ajanaku.
To Lawrence's right is his assistant, Adebayo.

Below, dance inaugurating the costumes.
Uzairue, Jattu, 4 February 1973

'Ancient Mother'
masquerade costume
and headdress
by Lawrence Ajanaku
Cotton, wool and appliqué
Northern Edo, Nigeria
1973
Fowler Museum of
Cultural History
University of California
Los Angeles

Cotton and
viscose textile
Asante, Ghana
20th century
Collection Marine Biras

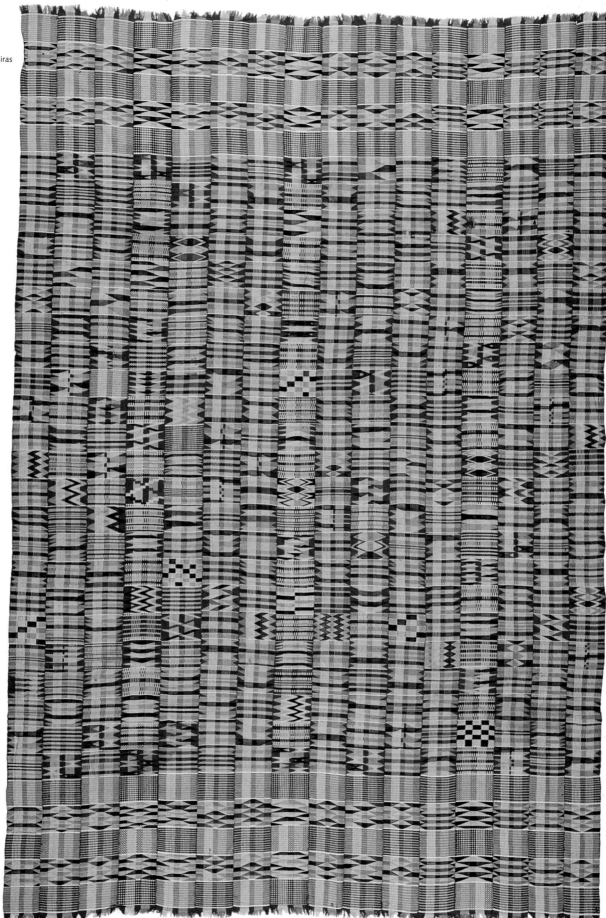

Silk textile
(*nsaduaso*)
with warp-striped
pattern *Oyokoman*
(the lineage of
the Asantehene)
and float-weave
in the *Adwinasa*
('Fullness
of Ornament')
manner
Asante, Bonwire,
Ghana,
late 19th century
Collection
Peter Adler

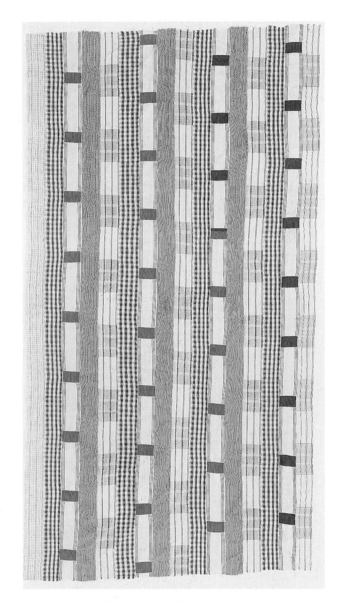

Cotton textile
Asante, Ghana
Early 20th century
Collection Peter Adler

Silk textile with alternating warp-faced and weft-faced striping
and float-weave motifs (*nsaduaso*)
Asante, Bonwire, Ghana, 20th century
Collection Peter Adler

Cotton textile with alternating warp-faced and weft-faced plain weave
and supplementary weft floats (*adanudo*), Ewe, Kpetoe, Ghana, early 20th century
Collection Peter Adler

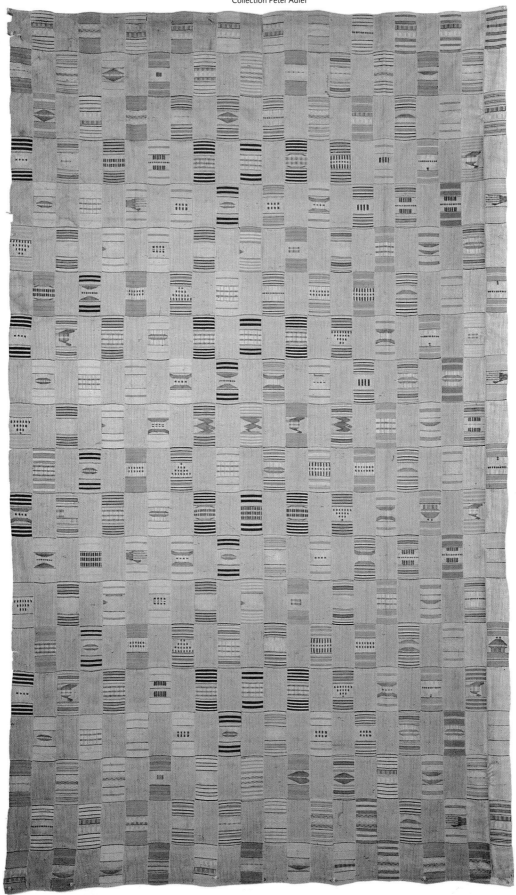

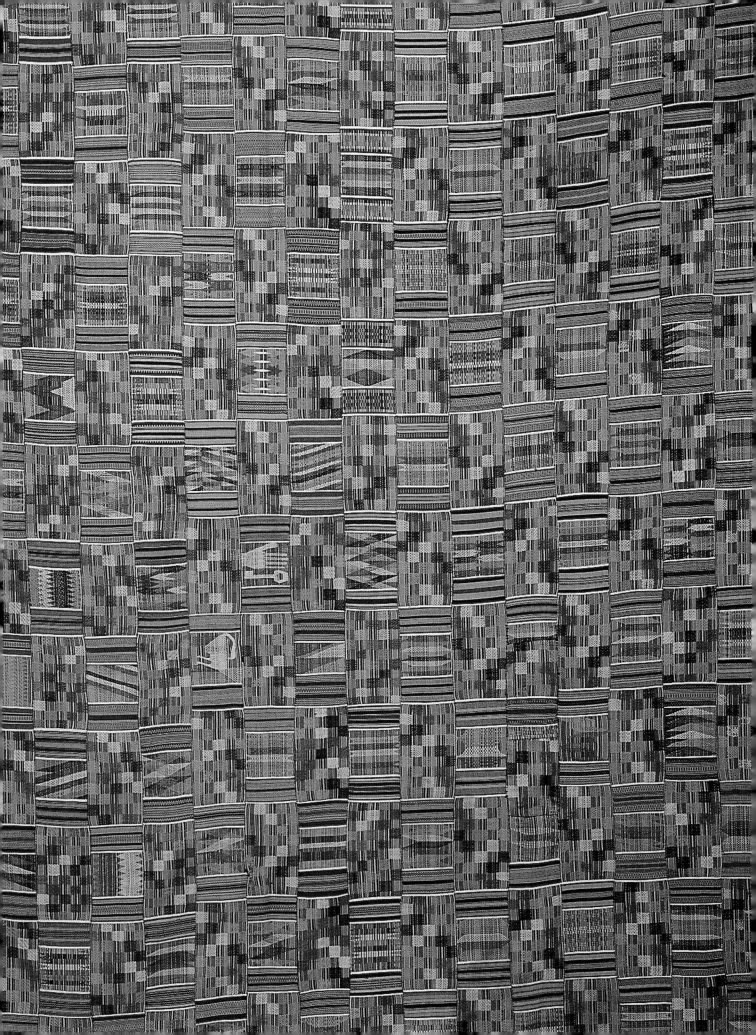

Cotton textile
with alternating
warp-faced and
weft-faced plain weave
and supplementary
weft floats
(*adanudo*)
(detail)
Ewe, Ghana
Early 20th century
Collection Peter Adler

Cotton textile with
alternating warp-faced
and weft-faced plain weave
and supplementary
weft floats (*adanudo*)
Ewe, Kpetoe, Ghana,
early 20th century
Collection Peter Adler

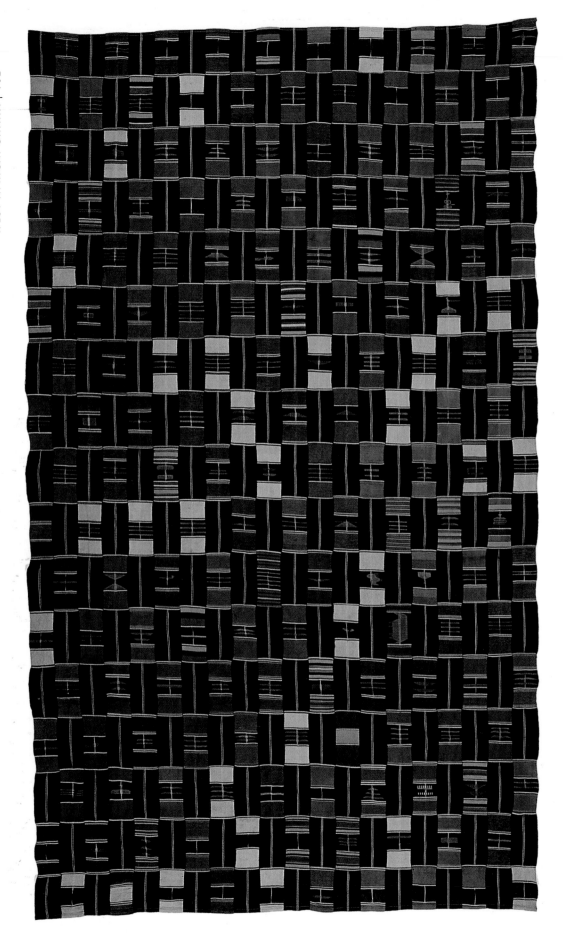

Cotton textile
with alternating warp-faced
and weft-faced plain weave
and supplementary weft floats
(*adanudo*)
Ewe, Kpetoe, Ghana
early 20th century
Collection Peter Adler

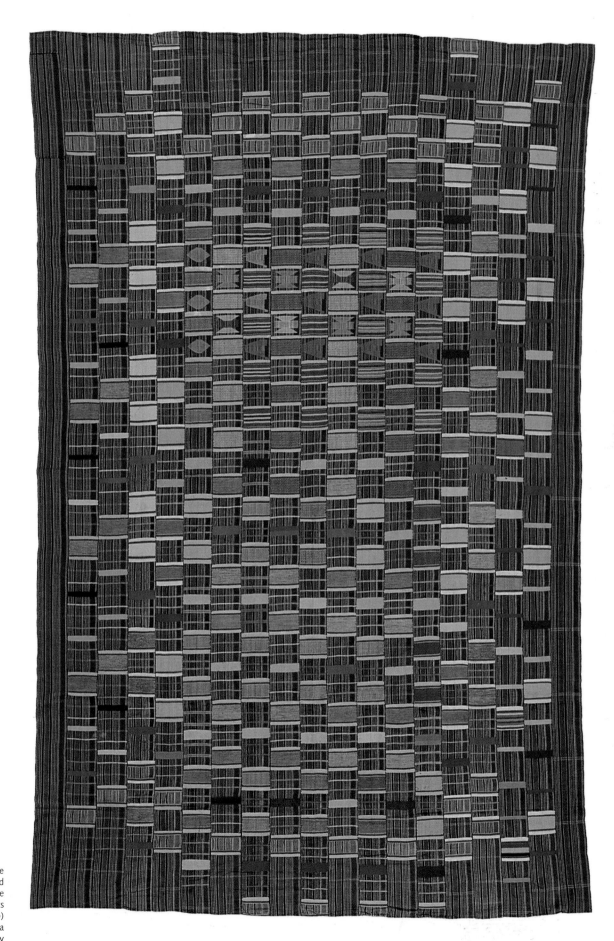

Cotton textile
with alternating warp-faced
and weft-faced plain weave
and supplementary weft floats
(*adanudo*)
Ewe, Kpetoe, Ghana
early 20th century
Collection Peter Adler

Flag, imported cotton appliqué for a military company (*asafo*)
Fante, Ghana, *c.*1950
Proverb: 'Fish grow fat for the benefit of the crocodile (who rules the river)'
Collection Peter Adler

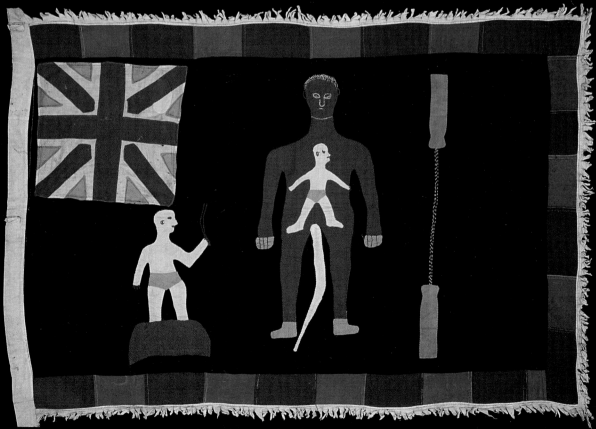

Flag, imported cotton appliqué for a military company (*asafo*)
Fante, Ghana, *c.*1900
Collection Peter Adler

Flag, imported cotton appliqué for a military company (*asafo*)
Fante, Ghana, c.1920
Proverb associated with dragon may be 'Will you fly or will you vanish?
Either way you can't escape us' – a challenge to rivals
Collection Peter Adler

Flag, imported cotton appliqué for a military company (*asafo*)
Sewn by Kweku Kakanu, Ekumpuanu, Kyirem No.1 Co., Fante, Ghana, c.1957
Proverb: 'Will you fly or will you vanish? Either way you can't escape us.'
Fowler Museum of Cultural History, University of California, Los Angeles

Embroidered cotton gown
Bamenda, Cameroon
July 1960
Collection J. R. Austin

Cotton *kanga*
Kitsutu design
Printed by Rivatex
Eldoret, Kenya
1995
Collection
Julia Hilger

Cotton *kanga*, '*Tujitahidi kulima njaa isitufisidi*'
('Let's try to harvest so that hunger does not harm/kill us')
Bizanje EUDK, ASP, Zanzibar, *c.*1950s-60s
Collection Barbara Gunnell

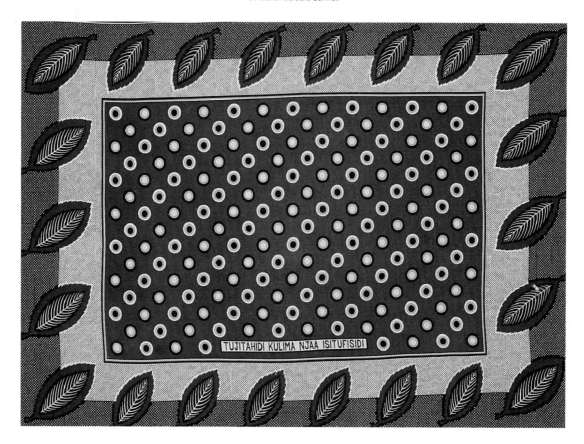

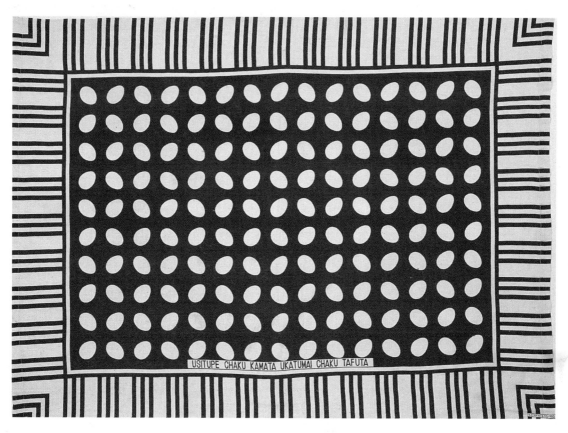

Cotton *kanga*, '*Usitupe chakukamata ukatumai cha kutafuta*'
('A bird in the hand is worth two in the bush') *c.*1970s
Collection Julia Hilger

Cotton *kanga,* design by Fatma Abdullah
'Ashante gari ya muhishimawa wete' ('Hurrah to the car of the President')
Printed by Atlas, India, for export to East Africa, 1980s
Collection Julia Hilger

Cotton *kanga*
'Maziwa ya mama ni tamu' ('Mothers' milk is sweet')
Printed by Rivatex, Eldoret, Kenya, *c.*1960
Collection Barbara Gunnell

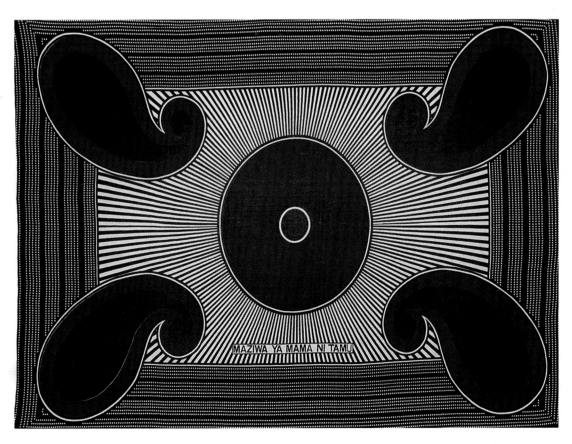

Wrap-around cloth (*nceka*)
Cloth, safety pins, mirrors, beads and brass chain
Tsonga, Northern Transvaal, South Africa, acquired 1987
Standard Bank Collection
University of the Witwatersrand
Johannesburg

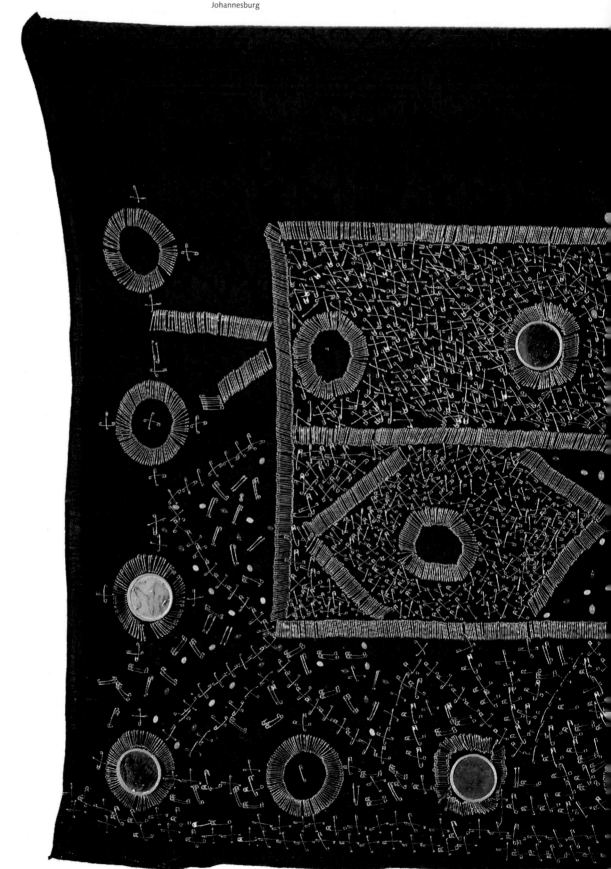

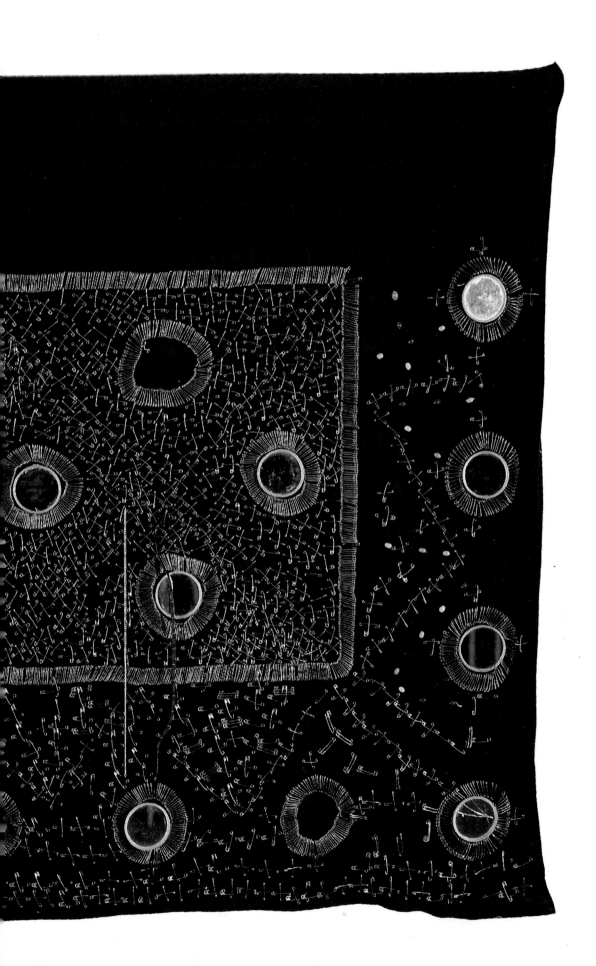

Beaded blanket (*irari*)
Standard Bank Collection, University of the Witwatersrand, Johannesburg

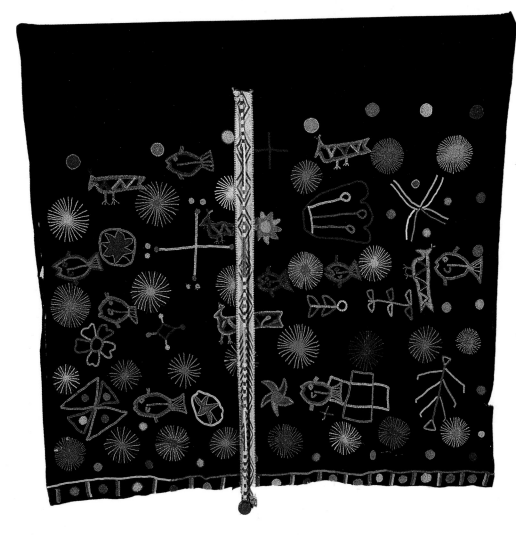

Wrap-around cloth (*nceka*)
Cloth and beads with snuff container
Tsonga-Shangana, Northern Transvaal, acquired 1994
Standard Bank Collection, University of the Witwatersrand, Johannesburg

Back apron (*sikomoka*)
Beads and cloth
Tonga, Kariba area, Zimbabwe, acquired 1989
Standard Bank Collection, University of the Witwatersrand
Johannesburg

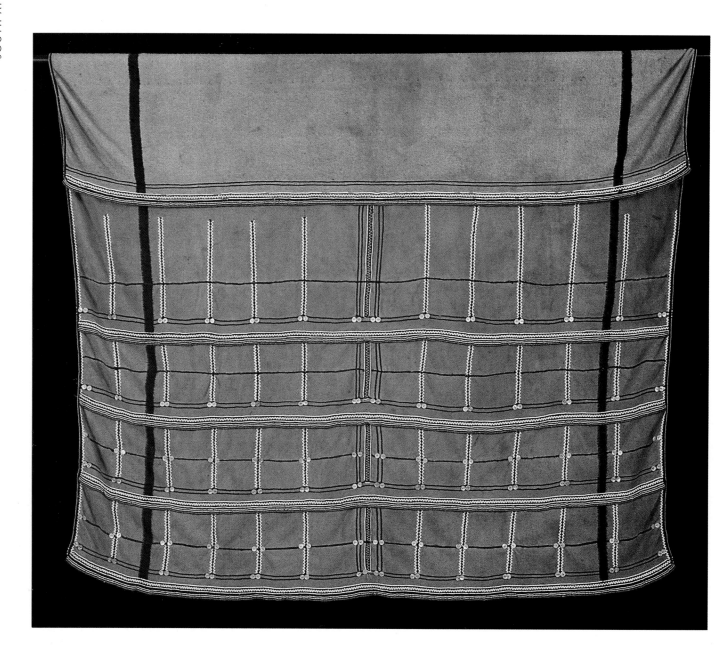

Woman's blanket (*ibhayi*)
Wool cloth, buttons and beads
Xhosa, South Africa, *c.*1950
Private collection

Remember our Fallen Comrades, for Chris Hani
by Sandra Kriel
Embroidery, photocopies and mixed media on cloth, 1993
Collection the artist

Aminata Diabaté, merchant,
wearing factory-printed variant of 'Hands and Fingers' design
at her stall in Brobo market, Ivory Coast, 1992

Wax print (*ie* resin-resist)
cotton textile
'The Lamp' design
Engraved and printed by
Haarlem Cotton Company
for E. Brown Flemming,
Glasgow
Early 20th century
Collection A. Brunnschweiler & Co.
Hyde

Wax print (*ie* resin-resist)
cotton textile
'Sword of Kingship'
or 'Corkscrew' design
Haarlem Cotton Company
for E. Brown Flemming,
Glasgow
in production by 1904
Collection A. Brunnschweiler & Co.
Hyde

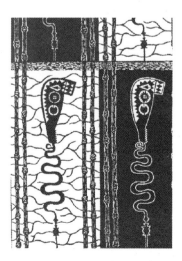

Drawing for
more recent engraving
of 'Sword of Kingship'
design
Collection A. Brunnschweiler & Co.
Hyde

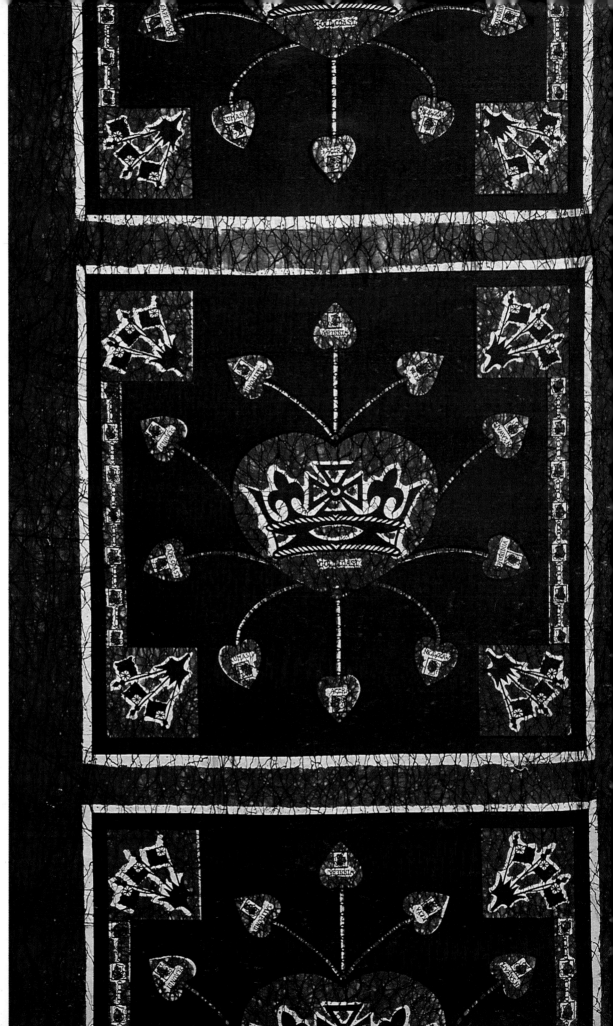

Fancy print
cotton textile
'Nana Prempeh,
Asantehene'
Printed at
Newton Bank
Works for
United Africa
Company
*c.*1929
Collection
Brian Anderton

Wax print (*ie* resin-resist)
cotton textile
'Postal' design featuring stamps
for ports of colonial Gold Coast.
Haarlem Cotton Company/
E. Brown Flemming, Glasgow,
in production by 1905
Collection
A. Brunnschweiler & Co.,
Hyde

Fancy print cotton textile
Commemorative design
Coronation 1937 and life story
of King George VI
Printed at Rhodes Works
(Calico Printers Association)
by S. Schwabe & Co.
probably for United Africa Company
20th century
Collection Brian Anderton

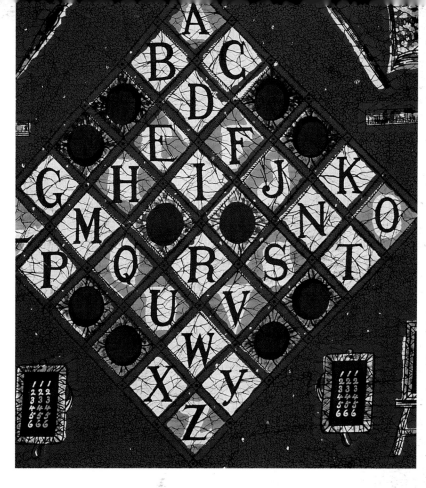

Wax print (*ie* resin-resist)
cotton textile
'Alphabet' design
Probable
Haarlem Cotton Company design
for E. Brown Flemming, Glasgow,
in production early 20th century
Collection A. Brunnschweiler & Co.
Hyde

Wax print (*ie* resin resist)
cotton textile
'Staircase' design
(relates to power, authority,
chiefly and royal status and,
through death, to heaven)
Probable original
Haarlem Cotton Company design
for E. Brown Flemming, Glasgow
Early 20th century
Collection A. Brunnschweiler & Co.
Hyde

Wax print (*ie* resin-resist) cotton textile
Imitation of 1935 Jubilee *adire* design
Printed by Uniwax, Ivory Coast,
acquired Adjamé market,
Abidjan, Ivory Coast, 1989
Collection K. Bickford

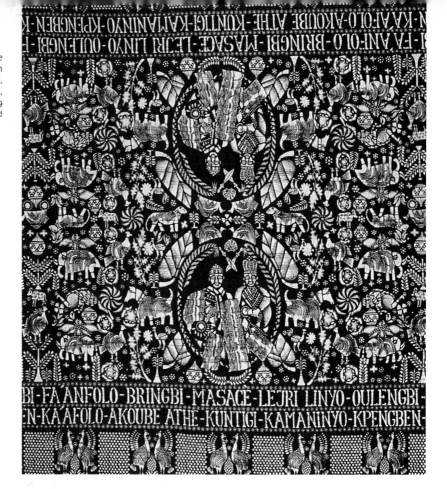

Wax print cotton textile
Imitation *adinkra*
Acquired *c.*1989
Collection Afrograph

Wax print (*ie* resin-resist) cotton textile, Commemorative design
2nd World Black and African Festival of Arts and Culture (FESTAC),
Lagos, Nigeria, 1977
Printed at Newton Bank Works for A. Brunnschweiler & Co.
and sold to SGGG Togo in transit to Nigeria
Collection Brian Anderton

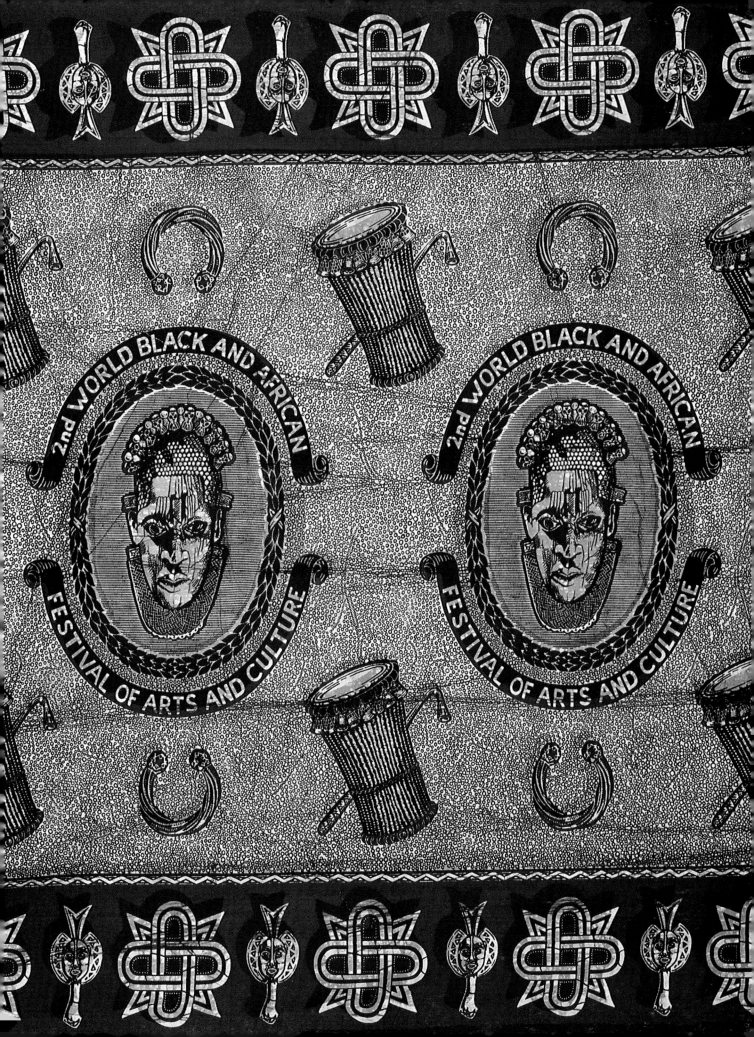

Fancy print
cotton textile
'Cooling Fans' design
Printed by Faso Fani
Burkina Faso
1990s
The Newark Museum
New Jersey

Wax print (ie resin-resist)
cotton textile
'Faso Tours' design
Printed by Faso Fani
Burkina Faso, c.1987
The Newark Museum
New Jersey

Wax print (ie resin-resist)
cotton textile
Printed by
Akosombo Textiles Ltd,
Akosombo, Ghana
acquired Kumasi, Ghana
1995
Collection
John and Susan Picton

Fancy print cotton textile
'*Owu Se Fie*' ('Death spoils the family') design
Acquired Ghana, 1994
Collection John and Susan Picton

Fancy print cotton textile
'*La Mort est pénible*' ('Death is hard') design
Printed by Utexi, Ivory Coast
Acquired Bouaké market, Abidjan, Ivory Coast, 1992
Collection K. Bickford

Wax print (*ie* resin-resist) cotton textile
'Children are better than money' design
Printed at Nichem, Nigeria, acquired Bouaké market,
Abidjan, Ivory Coast, 1992
Collection K. Bickford

Fancy print cotton textile
'*Si je savais*' ('If I'd known') design
Printed by ITEMA, Bamako, Mali, 1980s
Collection ITEMA

Wax print (*ie* resin resist)
cotton textile
Commemorative design
President Senghor and
Senegalese Independence
Printed by Newton Bank Works
for Grafton African
*c.*1960
Collection Brian Anderton

Fancy print cotton textile
Nelson Mandela design
for ANC campaign
in first democratic election
South Africa 1994
Private collection

Fancy print cotton textile
Printed by ITEMA
Bamako, Mali, 1980s
Collection ITEMA

Fancy print cotton textile
'Ce que femme veut'
('What women want') design
Ivory Coast, 1980s
The Newark Museum
New Jersey

Wax print (*ie* resin-resist) cotton textile
'Hands and Fingers' design
Printed at Newton Bank Works for A. Brunnschweiler & Co.
Collection of A. Brunnschweiler & Co.
Hyde

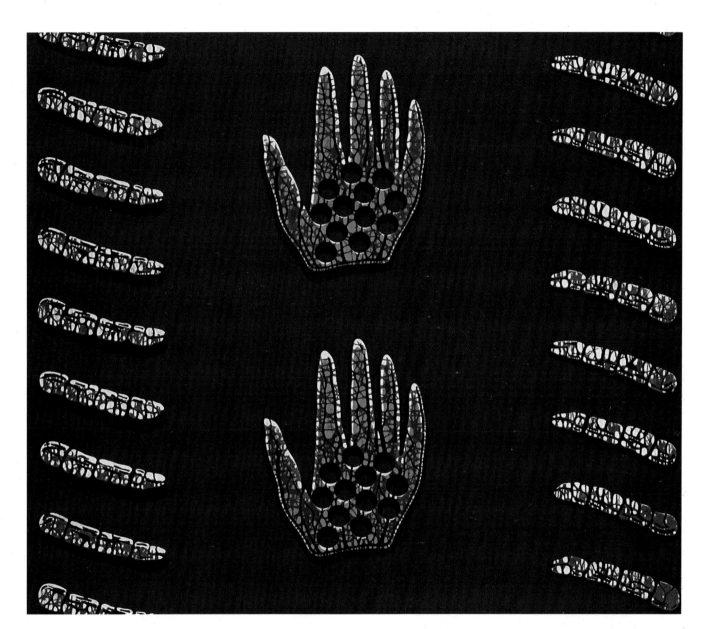

Adams, M. 1978
'Kuba embroidered cloth', *African Arts*, vol.XII, no.1

Adler, P. and Barnard, N. 1982
African Majesty: The Textile Art of the Ashanti and Ewe, Thames and Hudson Ltd, London

Adler, P. and Barnard, N. 1992
Asafo! African Flags of the Fante, Thames and Hudson Ltd, London

Aherne, T.D. 1992
Nakunte Diarra: Bògòlanfini Artist of the Beledougou, exh. cat., Indiana University Art Museum, Bloomington

Anderton, B., n.d.
Unpublished papers, Arthur Brunnschweiler & Co., Hyde, Cheshire

Aniakor, C. 1978
'The Igbo Ijele mask', *African Arts*, vol.XI, no.4

Aronson, L. 1980a
'History of cloth trade in the Niger Delta: A study of diffusion' in *Textiles of Africa* (Idiens, D. and Ponting, K.G. eds), Pasold Research Fund, Bath

Aronson, L. 1980b
'Patronage and Akwete weaving', *African Arts*, vol.XIII, no.3, pp.62-6, 91

Aronson, L. 1982
'Popo weaving: The dynamics of trade in Southeastern Nigeria', *African Arts*, vol.XV, no.3, pp.43-7, 90-1

Aronson, L. 1984
'Women in the Arts' in *African Women South of the Sahara* (Hay, J.M. and Stichter, S. eds), Longman, London

Aronson, L. 1989
'Akwete weaving, tradition and change' in *Man Does Not Go Naked* (Engelbrecht, B. and Gardi, B. eds), Museum für Völkerkunde, Basel

Aronson, L. 1992
'Ijebu Yoruba *Aso Olona*: A contextual and historical overview', *African Arts*, vol.XXV, no.3

Barbour, J. 1970
'Nigerian "Adire" cloths', *Baessler-Archiv*, vol.XVIII

Barbour, J. 1971
'The origin of some *adire* designs' in *Adire Cloth in Nigeria* (Barbour, J., and Simmonds, D. eds), Ibadan

Barbour, J. and Simmonds, D. (eds) 1971
Adire Cloth in Nigeria, The Institute of African Studies, University of Ibadan

Bedford, E. (ed.) 1993
Ezakwantu, Beadwork from the Eastern Cape, exh. cat., South African National Gallery, Cape Town

Beier, U. (ed.) 1991
Thirty Years of Oshogbo Art, Iwalewa House, Bayreuth

Bickford, K. 1994
'The A.B.C.'s of Cloth and Politics in Côte d'Ivoire', *Africa Today*, 2nd Quarter

Bogolan et arts graphiques du Mali, 1990, exh. cat., Museé National des Arts Africains et Océaniens, Paris/ Editions ADEIAO, Paris

Borgatti, J. 1976
'Okpella masking traditions', *African Arts*, vol.IX, no.4

Borgatti, J. 1979
From the Hands of Lawrence Ajanaku, Fowler Museum of Cultural History, University of California, Los Angeles

Borgatti, J. 1983
Cloth as Metaphor: Nigerian Textiles from the Museum of Cultural History, University of California, Los Angeles

Boser-Sarivaxévanis, R. 1969
Aperçus sur la teinture à l'indigo en Afrique Occidentale, Basle

Boser-Sarivaxévanis, R. 1972a
Textilhandwerk in Westafrika, Basle

Boser-Sarivaxévanis, R. 1972b
Les tissus de l'Afrique Occidentale, Pharos-Verlag Hansrudolf Schwabe, Basle

Boser-Sarivaxévanis, R. 1975
Recherche sur l'histoire des textiles traditionnels tissés et teints de L'Afrique Occidentale, Basle

Boser-Sarivaxévanis, R. November 1983
'African textiles', *Swissair Gazette*

Boston, J.S. 1960
'Some northern Ibo masquerades', *Journal of the Royal Anthropological Institute*, vol.XC, no.1

Bray, J.M. 1968
'The organisation of traditional weaving in Iseyin, Nigeria', *Africa*, vol.XXXVIII, no.3

Brommer, B. (ed.) 1989
Katoendruk in Nederland, exh.cat., Gemeentemuseum Helmond / Nederlands Textielmuseum, Tilburg

Brommer, B. (ed.) 1991
Bontjes voor de tropen: De export van imitatieweefsels naar de tropen, Uitgeverij Waanders bv, Zwolle/ Gemeentemuseum Helmond

Carreira, A. 1968
Panaria Cabo-Verdiano-Guineense: Aspectos históricos e sócio-económicos, Junta de Investigações do Ultramar, Lisbon

Césaire, A. 1939
Cahier d'un retour au pays natal, Paris

Clarke, J.D. 1938
'Ilorin weaving', *Nigeria Magazine*, no.14

Cole, H.M. and Aniakor, C.C. 1986
Igbo Arts: Community and Cosmos, Fowler Museum of Cultural History, University of California, Los Angeles

Cole, H.M. and Ross, D.H. 1977
The Arts of Ghana, Museum of Cultural History, University of California, Los Angeles

Cordwell, J. and Schwartz, R. (eds) 1979
The Fabrics of Culture, Mouton, The Hague

Crowning Achievements: African Arts of Dressing the Head, 1995 exh.cat., Fowler Museum of Cultural History, University of California, Los Angeles

Davison, P. and Harries, P. 1980
'Cotton weaving in south-east Africa: its history and technology' in *Textiles of Africa* (Idiens, D. and Ponting, D.G. eds) Pasold Research Fund, Bath

Deliss, C. (ed.) 1990
Lotte or the Transformation of the Object, exh.cat., Akademische Druck-u. Verlagsanstalt, Graz

Dodwell, C.B. 1955
'Iseyin, the town of Yoruba weavers', *Nigeria Magazine*, no.46

Domowitz, S. 1992, 'Wearing proverbs: Anyi names for printed factory cloth', *African Arts*, vol.XXV, no.3

Ebong, I. 1991
'Negritude: between mask and flag - Senegalese cultural ideology and the École de Dakar' in *Africa Explores*, exh.cat., The Center for African Art, New York, and Prestel, Munich

Echeruo, M.J.C. 1977
Victorian Lagos, London

Eicher, J.B. 1969
African Dress: A Select and Annotated Bibliography of Sub-Saharan Countries, East Lansing

Eicher, J.B. 1976
Nigerian Handcrafted Textiles, University of Ife Press, Ife-Ife, Nigeria

Emery, I. 1966
The Primary Structures of Fabrics, Textile Museum, Washington DC

Ene, J.C. 1964
'Indigenous silk-weaving in Nigeria', *Nigeria Magazine*, no.81

Erekosina, T. and Eicher, J.B. 1981
'Kalabari cut thread and pulled thread cloth', *African Arts*, vol.XIV, no.2

Etienne-Nugue, J. and Laget, E. 1990
Ivory Coast Handicrafts: Traditional Handicrafts in Black Africa, Institut Culturel Africain, Senegal

Findlay, B. 1995
'Aspects of Cloth Usage and Adaptation among the Tsonga-Shangana Women of the Northern Transvaal', unpublished MA thesis, University of Natal, Pietermaritzburg

Geary, C.M. and Nicolls, A. 1992
Elmina: Art and Trade on the West African Coast, Smithsonian Institution Press, Washington and London

Gilfoy, P.S. 1987
Patterns of Life: West African Strip-Weaving Traditions, National Museum of African Art, Washington DC

Goody, E.N. (ed.) 1982
From Craft to Industry: The Ethnography of Proto-Industrial Cloth Production, Cambridge University Press, Cambridge

Hammond-Tooke, D. and Nettleton, A. (eds) 1989

Ten Years of Collecting (1979-1989), University of the Witwatersrand, Johannesburg

Heathcote, D. 1972a
'Hausa embroidered dress', *African Arts*, vol.V, no.2

Heathcote, D. 1972b
'A Hausa embroiderer of Katsina', *The Nigerian Field*, vol.XXXVII, no.3

Heathcote, D. 1972c
'Some Hausa lizard designs', *Embroidery*, vol.XXIII, no.4,

Heathcote, D. 1972d
'Insight into a creative process: A rare collection of embroidery drawings from Kano', *Savanna*, vol.I, no.2

Heathcote, D. 1973a
'A selection of Hausa children's fashions', *The Nigerian Field*, vol.XXXVIII, no.3

Heathcote, D. 1973b
'Hausa women's dress in the light of two recent finds', *Savanna*, vol.II, no.1

Heathcote, D. 1974a
'Aspects of style in Hausa embroidery', *Savanna*, vol.III, no.1

Heathcote, D. 1974b
'A Hausa charm gown', *Man*, vol.IX, no.4

Heathcote, D. 1974c
'Hausa embroidery stitches', *The Nigerian Field*, vol.XXXIX, no.4

Heathcote, D. 1975
'Hausa hand-embroidered caps', *The Nigerian Field*, vol.XL, no.2

Heathcote, D. 1976a
The Arts of the Hausa, exh. cat., World of Islam Festival, Commonwealth Institute, London

Heathcote, D. 1976b
'A *Shabka mai yanka* from Zaria', *Embroidery*, vol.XXVII, no.2

Heathcote, D. 1983
'Hausa machine embroidery', *Embroidery*, vol.XXXIV, no.4,

Hobsbawm, E. and Ranger, T. (eds) 1983
The Invention of Tradition, Cambridge University Press, Cambridge

Idiens, D. and Ponting, K.G. (eds) 1980
Textiles of Africa, Pasold Research Fund, Bath

Imperato, P.J. and Shamir, M. 1970
'Bogolanfini: Mud cloth of the Bamana of Mali', *African Arts*, vol.III, no.4

Irele, A. 1977
'Negritude – Philosophy of African being', *Nigeria Magazine*, no.122-123

Isichei, E. 1983
A History of Nigeria, Longman, Harlow

Jackson, G. 1971
'The devolution of the jubilee design' in *Adire Cloth in Nigeria* (Barbour, J. and Simmonds, D. eds), Ibadan

Johnson, M. 1972
'Manding Weaving', unpublished paper, Manding Conference, London

🦋 Johnson, M. 1973
'Cloth on the banks of the Niger', *Journal of the Historical Society of Nigeria*, vol.VI, no.4

🦋 Johnson, M. 1974
Cotton Imperialism', *African Affairs*, no.73

🦋 Johnson, M. 1976
'Calico caravans: the Tripoli-Kano trade after 1880', *Journal of African History*, vol.XVII, no.1

🦋 Johnson, M. 1978
'Technology, competition and African crafts' in *The Imperial Impact* (Dewey, C. and Hopkins, A.G. eds), Athlone Press, University of London, for the Institute of Commonwealth Studies, London

🦋 Johnson, M. 1980
'Cloth as money: The cloth strip currencies of Africa' in *Textiles of Africa* (Idiens, D. and Ponting, K.G. eds), Pasold Research Fund, Bath

🦋 Kasfir, S.L. 1984
'One tribe, one style? Paradigms in the historiography of African art', *History in Africa*, vol.II, pp.163-93

🦋 Kent, K.P. 1972
'West African decorative weaving', *African Arts*, vol.VI, no.1

🦋 Keyes-Adenaike, C. 1993
'*Adire*: Cloth, Gender and Social Change in Southwestern Nigeria, 1841-1991', unpublished PhD thesis, University of Wisconsin-Madison

🦋 Knight, N. and Priebatsch, S. 1983
Ndebele Images, Natalie Knight Productions, Johannesburg

🦋 Kroese, W.T. 1976
The Origin of the Wax Block Print on the Coast of West Africa, NV Uitegeverij Smit van 1876 Hengelo

🦋 Kwami, A. 1994
'Textile Design in Ghana', unpublished report

🦋 Lamb, V. 1975a
West African Weaving, Duckworth, London

🦋 Lamb, V. and Lamb, A. 1975b
The Lamb Collection of West African Narrow Strip Weaving, Halifax

🦋 Lamb, V. 1980
'The classification and distribution of horizontal treadle looms in sub-Saharan Africa' in *Textiles of Africa* (Idiens, D. and Ponting, K.G. eds), Pasold Research Fund, Bath

🦋 Lamb, V. and Holmes, J. 1980
Nigerian Weaving, Roxford, Hertingfordbury, Hertfordshire

🦋 Lamb, V. and Lamb, A. 1981
Au Cameroun: Weaving-Tissage, Roxford Books, Hertingfordbury, Hertfordshire

🦋 Lamb, V. and Lamb, A. 1984
Sierra Leone Weaving, Roxford Books, Hertingfordbury, Hertfordshire

🦋 Levy, D. 1989
'Ndebele Beadwork' in *Ten Years of Collecting*, University of the Witwatersrand Art Galleries, Johannesburg

🦋 Levy, D. 1990
'Continuities and Change in Ndebele Beadwork: c.1883 to the Present', unpublished MA thesis, University of the Witwatersrand, Johannesburg

🦋 Linnebuhr, E. 1994
Sprechende Tücher, Frauenkleidung der Swahili (Ostafrika), Linden-Museum, Stuttgart

🦋 Mack, J. and Spring, C. 1991
African Textile Design, exh.cat., National Museum of Modern Art, Kyoto

🦋 Menzel, B. 1972
Textilien aus Westafrika, 3 vols, Museum für Völkerkunde, Berlin

🦋 Miller, J. von D. 1974
Art in East Africa, Frederick Muller Ltd, London

🦋 Nadel, S.F. 1942
A Black Byzantium: The Kingdom of Nupe in Nigeria, Oxford University Press for the International African Institute, London

🦋 Neilsen, R. 1979
'The history and development of wax-printed textiles intended for West Africa and Zaire' in *The Fabrics of Culture* (Cordwell, J. and Schwartz, R. eds), Mouton, The Hague

🦋 Nettleton, A.C.E. 1986
University Art Galleries' Collection of African Art, and selected works from the University Ethnological Museum Collection, exh. cat., University of the Witwatersrand, Johannesburg

🦋 Nettleton, A.C.E. and Becker, R. 1989
'Tsonga-Shangana beadwork and figure' in *Ten Years of Collecting*, University of the Witwatersrand Art Galleries, Johannesburg

🦋 Nicklin, K. and Salmons, J. 1984
'Cross River Art Styles', *African Arts*, vol.XVIII, no.1

🦋 Noy, I. 1992
The Art of the Weya Women, Baobab Books, Harare

🦋 Oguntona, T., 1986
Basic Textiles: Design Concepts and Methods, Ahmadu Bello University, Zaria

🦋 Okeke, C.G. 1976
'Tradition and change in Igbo woven designs', *Nigeria Magazine*, no.121

🦋 Olaniyi-Davies, N. 1991, *Nike Olaniyi-Davies*, Iwalewa Haus, Bayreuth

🦋 Oyelola, P. 1995
'Textiles in Nigeria', unpublished report

🦋 Pallinder, A. 1990
'Adegboyega Edun: black Englishman and Yoruba cultural patriot' in *Self-assertion and Brokerage: Early Cultural Nationalism in West Africa* (de Moraes Farias, P.F. and Barber K. eds), pp.11-34, Centre of West African Studies, Birmingham University

🦋 Patterson, R. 1957
'Spinning and weaving' in *A History of Technology*, vol.III (Singer, C., Holmyard, E.J., et al eds), Oxford

🦋 Perani, J. 1992
'The cloth connection: Patrons and producers of Hausa and Nupe prestige strip-weave' in *History, Design and Craft in African Strip-woven Cloth*, Smithsonian Institution Press, Washington and London

🦋 Picton, J. 1980
'Women's weaving: The manufacture and use of textiles among the Igbirra people of Nigeria' in *Textiles of Africa* (Idiens, D. and Ponting, K.G. eds), Pasold Research Fund, Bath

🦋 Picton, J. 1990
'Transformations of the artifact: John Wayne, plastic bags, and the eye-that-surpasses-all-other-eyes' in *Lotte or the Transformation of the Object* (Deliss, C. ed.), Akademische Druck-u. Verlagsanstalt, Graz

🦋 Picton, J. 1992
'Tradition, technology and lurex: Some comments on textile history and design in West Africa' in *History, Design and Craft in West African Strip-woven Cloth*, Smithsonian Institution Press, Washington and London

🦋 Picton, J. and Mack, J. 1989
African Textiles, 2nd edition, British Museum Publications Ltd

🦋 Posnansky, M. 1992
'Traditional cloth from the Ewe heartland' in *History, Design and Craft in West African Strip-woven Cloth*, Smithsonian Institution Press, Washington and London

🦋 Powell, I. 1995
Ndebele: A People and their Art, Struik, Cape Town

🦋 Rattray, R.S. 1927
Religion and Art in Ashanti, Clarendon Press, Oxford

🦋 Renne, E. 1995
(forthcoming publication)

🦋 Ross, D.H. 1979
Fighting with Art: Appliquéd Flags of the Fante Asafo, Museum of Cultural History, University of California, Los Angeles, Pamphlet Series, vol.1, no.5

🦋 Salmons, J. 1980
'Funerary shrine cloths of the Annang Ibibio, South-east Nigeria', *Textile History*, vol.XI

🦋 Salmons, J. 1985
'Martial arts of the Annang', *African Arts*, vol.XIX, no.1

🦋 Shaw, T. 1977
Unearthing Igbo-Ukwu, Ibadan

🦋 Sieber, R. 1972
African Textiles and Decorative Arts, Museum of Modern Art, New York

🦋 Smith, F. and Ficher, J. 1982
African Art

🦋 Spencer, A.M. 1982
In Praise of Heroes: Contemporary African Commemorative Cloth, Newark Museum, New Jersey

🦋 Spring, C. 1989
African Textiles, Bracken Books, London

🦋 Stanfield, N. 1971
'Dyeing methods in Western Nigeria' in *Adire Cloth in Nigeria* (Barbour, J. and Simmonds, D. eds), Ibadan

🦋 de Stefano, E.A.
Threads of Life: A Journey in Creativity, Ramses Wissa Wassef Art Centre, Egypt

🦋 Steiner, C. 1985
'Another image of Africa: toward an ethnohistory of European cloth marketed in West Africa 1873-1960', *Ethnohistory*, vol.32, no.2

🦋 Storey, J. 1974
Textile Printing, Thames and Hudson Ltd, London

🦋 Storey, J. 1978, *Manual of Dyes and Fabrics*, Thames and Hudson Ltd, London

🦋 Tall, P.I. 1975
'Situation de l'artiste Négro-Africain contemporain' in *Art Nègre et Civilisation de l'Universel*, Nouvelles Editions Africaines, Dakar

🦋 *Textile History*, vol.II, 1980
(Also published as *Textiles of Africa*, Idiens, D. and Ponting, K.G. eds, Pasold Research Fund, Bath)

🦋 Till, C. (et al) 1983
Zimbabwe Crafts: The Metal Box Crafts Exhibition, The National Gallery of Zimbabwe, Harare

🦋 Vail, L. (ed.) 1989
The Creation of Tribalism in Southern Africa, James Currey, London

🦋 Wahlman, M. and Chuta, E. 1979
'Sierra Leone resist-dyed textiles' in *The Fabrics of Culture* (Cordwell, J. and Schwartz, R. eds), Mouton, The Hague

🦋 Weiner, A.B. and Schneider, J. (eds) 1989
Cloth and Human Experience, Smithsonian Institution Press, Washington and London

🦋 *Yoruba Textiles: West African Cloth Culture*, 1992
exh. cat., Craftspace Touring, Birmingham

GLOSSARY

For further details of techniques, see John Picton and John Mack, *African Textiles*, British Museum Publications, 1989

adanudo : lit. skilled cloth, made by Ewe-speaking peoples of southern Ghana and Togo. Cloth with alternating warp- and weft-faced patterns made up of narrow strips woven by hand on a double-heddle loom and sewn together by hand or machine.

adinkra : cloth of plain textile onto which originally non-figurative emblems with proverbial connotations are printed with a black pigment using stamps cut from pieces of calabash. Production is concentrated upon Ntonso, near Kumasi, Ghana.

adire : Yoruba term for indigo resist-dyed cloth, Nigeria. There are two basic types: *adire eleko,* where the resisting agent is starch which may be painted on by hand and/or through a stencil of metal, or applied by comb (which gives a pattern of parallel lines); and *adire oniko,* where cloth is stitched or tied with raffia or thread, sometimes around sticks or stones to create different patterns.

adwinasa : lit. fullness of ornament (*adwini*, ornament, motif, artifice). Cloth (often made of silk in the late nineteenth century) made up of narrow strips woven by hand on a double-heddle loom and sewn together, Asante, Ghana. The basic weft-faced pattern was minimised and the entire face of the cloth embellished with float-weave patterns. The most complex *adwinasa*, where there is no exact repetition of a pattern, were the most highly prized.

agbada : man's wide-sleeved gown, Yoruba, Nigeria; the equivalent in Hausa, Nigeria, is the *riga*.

ankh sign : Ancient Eygptian graphic sign for eternal life.

asafo : military companies, Fante, Ghana.

Asantehene : head of an Akan (Twi-speaking communities) kingdom. These kingdoms came into being in the seventeenth century, and made up the Asante confederation of kingdoms in Ghana.

asasia : silk cloth hand-woven only to the commission of the Asantehene. A loom with a third pair of heddles is used.

aso oke : from the Yoruba (Nigeria): *aso*, cloth; *oke*, hill, the top of something; *ie* high-status cloth. It is made up of narrow strips (usually four inches wide) of cotton or synthetic fibres, including viscose and lurex, that are hand-woven on horizontally mounted double-heddle looms and sewn together by hand or machine.

batik : Javanese term for wax-resist dyeing.

block printing : method of printing from a solid (or layered) block of wood with a relief of engraved wood. The basic design of the *kanga* of East Africa is related to Indian hand-block printing techniques. Hand-block printing is still used in factories in Europe producing cloth for export to Africa.

bogolan or *bogolanfini* : discharge-dyed cloth where the base cloth is dyed yellow, then painted with iron-rich mud which 'saddens' the yellow, burning it dark brown; the remaining yellow is then washed out with a caustic liquid agent.

broadloom : loom giving a broad width of cloth; until recent years most of the weaving by women in Nigeria was performed using a single-heddle broadloom in which only one set of warps is leashed.

chitenge or *kitenge* : term used in Central and East Africa for cloths worn around the waist falling to the ankles. Unlike the *kanga* and *kikoy*, they are printed in a continuous length. They are normally sold in two-metre lengths ready to be worn but are sometimes cut and made into garments.

cut-pile embroidery : form of embroidery practised by Kuba people, Zaire, where the base cloth is a rectangle of woven raffia which may be dyed before being embroidered or after the cloth is complete. Very fine raffia fibres which have been softened and dyed are used for the embroidery. The embroidery is the work of women; the weaving, that of men.

damask : also known as 'brocade', 'Guinea brocade', or 'Guinea' (Nigeria) and *sheddar* (Ghana).

double-heddle loom : used for weaving narrow strips of cloth, operated by the hands and feet. The heddles are joined to each other by a cord and operated by foot pedals; in depressing one pedal the other is raised.

duplex : term used for cloth printed on both sides, in the case of factory-printed textiles produced for, and in, Africa, imitating the effects of batik.

egungun : term used for Yoruba ancestral masquerading associations and masked performers, Nigeria.

fancy print : term used for factory-produced textiles printed on one face of the cloth only by engraved metal roller or rotary screen, also known by numerous other names, including 'imiwax', 'Java print' and 'roller print'.

green ground : term used for early twentieth-century fancy print technique used only in the UK. Cloth is printed by roller with red, yellow and a resist acid, followed by a pad of blue. The areas unprotected by resist acid change from red to plum, yellow to green, and white to blue.

grey cloth : unbleached cotton cloth.

heddle : a device that effects the separation of the warp to permit the passage of the weft.

ikat : threads that are tied before being dyed and are then woven.

indigo : plant which grows wild in West Africa and gives a deep blue dye.

irari : one of the terms used for a blanket worn around the shoulders by Ndebele people, South Africa.

ixakatho : blanket worn around the shoulders by Xhosa people of the eastern Cape, South Africa.

kampala : a Nigerian fashion named after the Kampala Peace Conference during the Nigerian Civil War when a form of wax resist-dyed cloth, in which molten candlewax is sprinkled over the cloth before dyeing, became popular.

kanga : lit. guinea fowl. Rectangular printed cloths worn in East Africa. Bought in pairs, one is worn around the waist, the other over the head and shoulders. Their design follows a convention which relates to the hand-block printing traditions of India and is characterised by a border on all four sides around a central area with a repeated pattern or singular motif.

kente : term conventionally used for a variety of decorative cloths from Ghana that are made up of hand-woven narrow strips, sewn together by hand or machine. The origin and etymology of the word are uncertain.

khasa : woollen blankets woven by the Maboube weavers of the inland delta region of the River Niger in Mali.

kikoy : term used in Southern Africa for plaid-patterned cloth.

kitsutu : one of the earliest known *kanga* designs, they are given to brides as part of their dowry to cast off evil. Unlike other *kanga*, the design includes borders along the two shorter ends of the cloth, not all four sides.

lamba : term used throughout Madagascar to denote the rectangular hand-woven cloth made of a wide range of materials (including plantain fibres, tree bark, raffia and bast as well as silk and synthetic fibres).

leso : handkerchiefs, originally imported to East Africa by the Portuguese and sewn together to make up a piece of cloth the size of the present-day *kanga*.

liphotho : Ndebele apron, often embellished with beadwork, South Africa.

lurex : synthetic element imported to Africa initially from Japan, now also manufactured in Africa.

minceka : plural of *nceka*, wrap-around skirts usually made by the Tsonga-speaking women of northern Transvaal, South Africa and worn in pairs. A pre-printed cloth is often used which is dyed deep blue and embellished with a wide range of materials including safety pins, thread, buttons, beads and mirrors.

Narmer palette : decorative form of palette used for grinding eye shadow (malachite) in Ancient Egypt which shows the unification of Egypt resulting from the conquest of Lower Egypt by Upper Egypt.

pagne : term used (primarily in the Francophone countries of West Africa) for a length of cloth used as a wrap-around skirt.

Popo : hand-woven cloth made in the Niger Delta that takes its name from the coastal communities of Grand and Little Popo.

raffia : plant fibre used particularly in Central African region to weave rectangular pieces of cloth.

rayon : synthetic fibre often described as 'silk' in West Africa; its use is now largely replaced by that of another synthetic fibre, viscose.

resist : method of preventing dye(s) from colouring cloth. Substances such as starch or wax may be used as a resist, also cloth may be stitched or tied to resist dye.

sadza : maize meal porridge used in the southern region of Africa as a form of resist which is painted onto cloth. Pigment is then applied between the *sadza* outlines. When the *sadza* is dry it is scraped off, and the cloth washed.

shabka : type of embroidered gown made in Nigeria which is characterised by an elaborate arrangement of squares and circles in a decorative scheme that has links with West African charm papers.

supplementary-weft float : yarn, thread or element extra to that used for warp and weft where it is not woven in with the weft in a straightforward over-and-under sequence, but in effect 'floats' freely across two or more warps before being reintegrated into the cloth.

warp : yarn, thread or other elements held in tension by the loom.

warp-faced : where the warp threads are concentrated together, consequently hiding the weft.

wax print : term used for factory-produced textiles printed on both faces of the cloth in an exact match using a resin-resist and imitating the effects of batik.

weft : the yarn, thread or other elements which interweave with the warp.

weft-faced : where the wefts hide the warp, *ie* where the warp threads are spread apart as they are mounted on the loom.

woven openwork : technique of weaving together groups of warps to create a pattern of holes.

LIST OF WORKS

Works are listed by country, medium and date. Length or height precedes width. Page numbers of illustrated works are given in square brackets.

EGYPT

1 ❦ Cotton appliqué by Salah El Din M. El Ozy [*p.61 detail*]
Commissioned for this exhibition, Egypt, 1995
365.8 x 378.5 cm
Inscription:
Say it to the one who knows it all
You might have learnt something, but many things have slipped you by!
Abu Nawas from *Diwan Abu Nawas*, Dar Hilal, Beirut, 1986, p.10
Translated by Abdullah al-Udhari

2 ❦ Hand-dyed cotton appliqué by Chant Avedissian [*p.61*]
1989-90
240 x 310 cm
Collection the artist

3 ❦ Hand-dyed cotton appliqué by Chant Avedissian
1989-90
240 x 220 cm
Collection the artist

4 ❦ Cotton textile with design based on Arabic script by Khamis Chehata
Screen-printed by hand
300 x 80 cm
*c.*1962
Collection the artist

SUDAN

5 ❦ Mahdist army cotton tunic
Northern Sudan, late 19th century
89 x 124 cm
Trustees of the British Museum
(1949 AF46.691)

CENTRAL AFRICA

6 ❦ Fabric coffin of imported blankets (*niombo*) [*p.57*]
Sundi-Kongo, early 20th century
180 cm high
Etnografiska Museet, Gothenburg, Sweden (1938.27.1)
Collected by E. Andersson

7 ❦ Fabric reliquary (*muzidi*) covered with factory-printed cotton
Bembe, Kolo, early 20th century
48 cm high
Etnografiska Museet, Gothenburg, Sweden (1938.23.31)
Collected by E. Andersson

8 ❦ Fabric reliquary (*muzidi*) covered with factory-printed cotton
Kongo, early 20th century
38 cm high
Collection Nadine and Raoul Lehuard

9 ❦ Raffia textile with cut-pile and cotton embroidery [*p.59*]
Kuba, Zaire, early 20th century
64.5 x 57.5 cm
Collection Peter Adler

10 ❦ Raffia textile with cut-pile embroidery
Kuba, Zaire, early 20th century
54 x 62 cm
Collection Peter Adler

11 ❦ Raffia textile with cut-pile embroidery
Kuba, Zaire, early 20th century
66 x 57 cm
Collection Peter Adler

12 ❦ Woven skirt, raffia with appliqué and cut-pile embroidery [*p.58*]
Kuba, Zaire, early 20th century
78.5 x 776 cm
Collection Peter Adler

13 ❦ Woven skirt, raffia with appliqué [*p.59*]
75 x 573 cm
Kuba, Zaire, 20th century
Collection Peter Adler

14 ❦ Woven skirt
Raffia with appliqué
Kuba, Zaire
115 x 619 cm
Collection Peter Adler

ZIMBABWE

15 ❦ Back apron (*sikomoka*), beads and cloth [*p.113*]
Tonga, Kariba area, acquired 1989
43.9 cm long
Standard Bank Collection, University of the Witwatersrand, Johannesburg (89.01.04.23)

SOUTH AFRICA

16 ❦ Beaded Middleburg blanket (*irari*) [*p.112*]
Ndebele, Central Transvaal, acquired 1986
87 cm long
Standard Bank Collection, University of the Witwatersrand, Johannesburg (86.01.02)

17 ❦ Married woman's apron (*liphotho*), vinyl, plastic, braid, rick-rack and other ready-made fabrics [*p.49*]
60.5 cm long
Ndebele, Central Transvaal, acquired 1985
Standard Bank Collection, University of the Witwatersrand, Johannesburg (85.35.03)

18 ❦ Married woman's apron (*liphotho*), canvas, beads, brass rings and fur
Ndebele, Central Transvaal, acquired 1988
51.4 cm long
Standard Bank Collection, University of the Witwatersrand, Johannesburg (88.02.011)

19 ❦ Wrap-around cloth (*nceka*), cloth, safety pins, mirrors, beads and brass chain [*pp.110-11*]
Tsonga, Northern Transvaal, acquired 1987
108 cm long
Standard Bank Collection, University of the Witwatersrand, Johannesburg (87.02.16)

20 ❦ Wrap-around cloth (*nceka*), cloth with beads and snuff container [*p.113*]
Tsonga-Shangana, Northern Transvaal, acquired 1994
190.4 x 132.3 cm
Standard Bank Collection, University of the Witwatersrand, Johannesburg (94.36.02)

21 ❦ Cloth with cotton embroidery and braid
Lobedu, Northern Transvaal, acquired 1992
81.8 x 154.2 cm
Standard Bank Collection, University of the Witwatersrand, Johannesburg (92.09.213)

22 ❦ Boy's blanket (*ixakatho*), wool, buttons, beads [*p.48*]
Xhosa, Fingo, Eastern Cape, acquired 1989
156 cm long
Standard Bank Collection, University of the Witwatersrand, Johannesburg (89.06.04)

23 ❦ Woman's blanket (*ibhayi*), wool cloth, buttons and beads [*p.114*]
Xhosa, *c.*1950
117 x 150 cm
Private collection

24 ❦ *Remember our Fallen Comrades, for Chris Hani* by Sandra Kriel [*p.115*]
Embroidery, photocopies and mixed media on cloth, 1993
94 x 94 cm
Collection the artist

25 ❦ *Remember our Fallen Comrades, for Thamy Mnyele* by Sandra Kriel
Embroidery, photocopies and mixed media on cloth, 1993
94 x 94 cm
Collection the artist

MADAGASCAR

26 ❦ Silk *lamba*
Madagascar, 1993
277 x 64 cm
Trustees of the British Museum (AF 1993 14.4)

MALI

27 ❦ Gown, cotton with silk embroidery [*pp.62-3*]
Ségou, *c.*1880
119 x 190 cm
Musée de l'Homme, Paris (80.69.8)

28 ❦ Indigo-dyed and embroidered cotton textile
Dogon, 20th century, acquired 1987
166 x 93 cm
Trustees of the British Museum (1987 AF7.20)

29 ❦ Narrow-strip blanket by Oumar Bocoum [*p.65*]
Machine-spun cotton, 1989
270 x 167 cm
Collection Marine Biras

30 ❦ Narrow-strip blanket, machine-spun cotton [*p.64*]
1994
227 x 160 cm
Private collection

31 ❦ Cotton gown stitch resist-dyed by Gogo Semega Maiga
Bamako, 1992
150 x 160 cm
Collection Aissa Dione

32 ❦ Cotton textile tie-dyed by Issa Bathily
1993
192 x 152 cm
Private collection

33 ❦ Cotton damask for gown tie-dyed by Gogo Semega Maiga [*p.70*]
'Fishbones' design
Bamako, 1994
334 x 167 cm
Private collection

34 ❦ Stitch resist-dyed cotton damask for gown [*p.70*]
Bamako, 1994
317 x 163 cm
Private collection

35 ❦ Tie-dyed cotton damask for gown [*p.70*]
Bamako, 1994
320 x 161 cm
Private collection

36 🕮 *Bogolan* ('mudcloth'), discharge-dyed narrow-strip cotton textile [*p.35*]
Rainy season, 1991
166 x 112 cm
Private collection

37 🕮 *La Traversée du Désert* (Crossing the Desert), by Alfousseini Kelly [*p.37*]
Bogolan ('mudcloth'), discharge-dyed canvas, 1993
91 x 147 cm
Collection the artist

NIGER

38 🕮 Embroidered textile
Peule, 1950
80 x 35 cm
Private collection

SENEGAL

39 🕮 *Couple d'enfants* by Mohamadou Zulu Mbaye [*p.34*]
Wool tapestry, maquette acquired 1977, edition no.7 made 1992
195 x 135 cm
Collection Manufactures Sénégalaises des Arts Décoratifs, Thiès

40 🕮 Narrow-strip cotton textile with viscose and lurex float-weave images of Pope Jean-Paul II [*p.66*]
Senegal, c.1992
Each strip 203 x 21 cm
Private collection

41 🕮 Samples of factory-woven broadloom cloth of cotton and raffia designed by Aissa Dione
Dakar, 1995
Each 300 x 90 cm
Collection the artist

42 🕮 Cotton stitch-resist indigo-dyed cotton damask
St Louis, 20th century
220 x 160 cm
Collection Aissa Dione

GUINEA BISSAU

43 🕮 Narrow-strip cotton textile [*p.66*]
Manjaka or Papel, early 20th century
206 x 105 cm
Trustees of the British Museum, Beving Collection (1934 3-7. 196)

44 🕮 Narrow-strip cotton textile
Manjaka or Papel, 20th century
184 x 117 cm
Trustees of the British Museum (1989 AF5.155)

SIERRA LEONE

45 🕮 Embroidered gown, indigo-dyed cotton [*detail p.67*]
c.1920
88 x 162 cm
Horniman Museum, London (27.7.55.9)

46 🕮 Tie-dyed cotton damask [*p.69*]
Kabala, acquired 1977
147 x 117 cm
Horniman Museum, London (1977.87)

47 🕮 Tie-dyed viscose textile [*p.69*]
Cloth purchased Liverpool, dyed Sierra Leone c.1990
184.8 x 148.5 cm
Collection Afrograph

IVORY COAST

48 🕮 Cotton textile tie-dyed in indigo and kola [*p.68*]
1970
165 x 110 cm
Private collection

NIGERIA

49 🕮 Man's gown, cotton with embroidery [*pp.72-3*]
Hausa(?), early 20th century
118 x 271 cm
Collection Peter Adler

50 🕮 Man's gown (*riga*), 'Eight Knives' design
Narrow-strip cotton and wild silk cloth in stripes of cream and beige with wild silk embroidery
Nupe, said to be from Bida, acquired Abiya, 1972
120 x 247 cm
Private collection

51 🕮 Man's gown (*riga*), *Shabka* design [*p.74*]
Factory-woven cotton with wild silk embroidery
Hausa, Kano, c.1950
151 x 300 cm
Private collection

52 🕮 Man's gown (*riga*), indigo-dyed hand-spun cotton with wild silk embroidery by Malam Suleiman [*pp.38, 75*]
'Eight Knives' design, version *Yar Ilori* ('Daughter of Ilorin')
Hausa, Zaria, 1973
154 x 265 cm
Private collection

53 🕮 Man's gown (*riga*), factory-woven imported cloth with green embroidery by Alhaji Sanni [*p.39*]
'Eight Knives' design, version *Yayin Sharif mai Wata* ('The Sharif fashion with a crescent moon')
Hausa, cloth purchased Zaria, embroidered Kano, 1974
146 x 233 cm
Private collection

54 🕮 Man's gown (*riga*), *Yar Kumasi* ('Daughter of Kumasi') design, embroidery stitched with Cornely-type machine on imported cotton damask [*p.76*]
Zaria, 1975
144 x 212 cm
Private collection

55 🕮 Man's lurex gown (*agbada*)
Yoruba, 1995
134.5 x 213 cm
Collection Nigerian Fabrics and Fashions, Brooklyn, New York and Ile-Oluji, Nigeria

56 🕮 King's crown, beads stitched to cotton over basketry base [*p.77*]
Yoruba, 20th century
79 cm high
Collection Peter Adler

57 🕮 King's crown, beads stitched to cotton over basketry base
Yoruba, 20th century
98 cm high
Collection Peter Adler

58 🕮 King's crown, beads stitched to cotton over basketry base
Yoruba, 20th century
102.5 cm high
Collection Peter Adler

59 🕮 *Egungun* costume, cloth, fibre and wood with thirteen Catholic devotional medals [*p.14*]
Ogbomoso, 20th century
150 cm high
Collection Eric Robertson, New York

60 🕮 Narrow-strip textile (*aso oke*), indigo-dyed hand- and machine-spun cotton with *ikat* stripes in the warp [*p.79*]
Yoruba, early 20th century
272 x 152 cm
Collection Judith Appio

61 🕮 Narrow-strip textile (*aso oke*), maroon cotton with green and blue rayon/viscose warp stripes
Yoruba, 1960s
194 x 144 cm
Collection Judith Appio

62 🕮 Narrow-strip red and white cotton textile (*aso oke*)
Yoruba, 1960s
230 x 137 cm
Collection K.P., Paris

63 🕮 Narrow-strip light brown and indigo cotton textile (*aso oke*)
Yoruba, 1960s
208 x 142 cm
Collection K.P., Paris

64 🕮 Narrow-strip textile (*aso oke*), off-white cotton with openwork and orange cotton supplementary weft-floats
Yoruba, mid-20th century
212 x 144 cm
Collection Judith Appio

65 🕮 Narrow-strip textile (*aso oke*), cotton with Qur'an board float-weave motifs [*p.11*]
Yoruba, mid-20th century
218 x 149 cm
Collection Judith Appio

66 🕮 Narrow-strip textile (*aso oke*) cotton with supplementary weft-float lettering [*p.80*]
Yoruba, 1960s
208 x 75 cm
Collection K.P., Paris

67 🕮 Narrow-strip textile (*aso oke*), cotton with supplementary weft-floats [*p.79*]
Yoruba, 1960s
181 x 151.5 cm
Collection Peter Adler

68 🕮 Narrow-strip textile (*aso oke*), cotton with openwork [*p.79*]
Yoruba, c.1970
237 x 74 cm
Collection Judith Appio

69 🕮 Narrow-strip textile (*aso oke*), grey and orange/brown cotton with openwork
Yoruba, 1970s
235 x 167 cm
Collection Marine Biras

70 🕮 Narrow-strip textile (*aso oke*), light brown and black cotton with gold lurex and openwork
Yoruba, c.1980
220 x 90 cm
Collection K.P., Paris

71 🕮 Narrow-strip textile (*aso oke*), cotton and lurex warp
Yoruba, c.1980
178 x 48 cm
Collection Judith Appio

72 ❦ Narrow-strip textile
(aso oke), gold lurex and white
cotton with openwork
Yoruba, 1990s
196 x 83 cm
Collection Elisha Renne

73 ❦ Narrow-strip textile
(aso oke), grey and blue lurex
Yoruba, 1993-4
124 x 183 cm
Collection Afrograph

74 ❦ Narrow-strip textile
(aso oke), cotton and lurex
with openwork
Yoruba, c.1980
227 x 79 cm
Collection Judith Appio

75 ❦ Narrow-strip textile
(aso oke), cotton, rayon
and lurex with openwork
and supplementary weft-floats
[p.79]
Yoruba, 1977
197 x 96.5 cm
Trustees of the National Museums
of Scotland, Edinburgh
(1978.500)

76 ❦ Narrow-strip textile
(aso oke), cotton and lurex with
openwork and supplementary
weft-floats [p.78]
Yoruba, 1977
194 x 103 cm
Trustees of the National Museums
of Scotland, Edinburgh
(1978.499)

77 ❦ Indigo tie-dyed cotton
textile (adire)
Yoruba, 20th century
221 x 174 cm
Collection Judith Appio

78 ❦ Indigo tie-dyed cotton
textile (adire)
Yoruba, 20th century
222 x 182 cm
Collection Judith Appio

79 ❦ Indigo stitch-resist and
tie-dyed cotton textile (adire)
[p.83]
Yoruba, 20th century
182 x 123 cm
Collection Judith Appio

80 ❦ Indigo tie-dyed cotton
textile (adire)
Yoruba, 20th century
216 x 185 cm
Collection Judith Appio

81 ❦ European double-warp
cotton textile with charioteers,
stitch-resist indigo-dyed (adire)
Yoruba, mid-20th century
190 x 118 cm
Collection Alec and Helen Travers

82 ❦ Indigo stitch-resist and
tie-dyed cotton textile (adire)
[p.81]
Yoruba, 20th century
186 x 156 cm
Collection Judith Appio

83 ❦ Indigo-dyed cotton cloth
(adire), Oloba (lit. 'that with a
king') design commemorating
the Silver Jubilee of the accession
of King George V and Queen
Mary in 1935 [p.16]
Starch-resist stencilled
and hand-painted
Yoruba, Abeokuta,
mid-20th century
201 x 86 cm
Private collection

84 ❦ Indigo starch resist-dyed
cotton cloth (adire) with
stencilled Oloba design intended
to commemorate the Coronation
of Edward VIII, 1936, based upon
that of his father's Silver Jubilee
[p.16]
Yoruba, Abeokuta,
mid-20th century
196 x 166 cm
Collection Alec and Helen Travers

85 ❦ Indigo starch resist-dyed
cotton textile (adire) with
stencilled lettering
'There is no king as God' design
[p.83]
Yoruba, 20th century
199 x 172 cm
Collection Judith Appio

86 ❦ Indigo starch resist-dyed
cotton textile (adire),
hand-painted Oloba design
commemorating the Silver Jubilee
of the accession of King George V
and Queen Mary in 1935
Yoruba, Ibadan, purchased
newly made, late 1960s
173.4 x 195.5 cm
Collection John and Susan Picton

87 ❦ Indigo starch resist-dyed
cotton textile (adire) with
hand-painted 'Ibadandun'
design [p.82]
Yoruba, 20th century
195 x 182 cm
Collection Judith Appio

88 ❦ Indigo starch resist-dyed
cotton textile (adire) with
hand-painted designs
Yoruba, 20th century
193 x 177 cm
Collection Judith Appio

89 ❦ Indigo starch resist-dyed
cotton textile (adire) with
hand-painted design of hands,
lettering, imitation stitch-resist
and tie-dyeing [p.83]
Yoruba, 1960s-1970s
183 x 170 cm
Collection Alec and Helen Travers

90 ❦ Tied, folded and stitched
resist-dyed cotton damask
(kampala)
Yoruba, Ibadan, acquired 1968
222 x 78 cm
Horniman Museum, London

91 ❦ Tie-dyed cotton textile
by Toyin Oguntona [p.71]
Zaria, 1994
526 x 130 cm
Private collection

92 ❦ My Village, embroidery
by Nike Olaniyi-Davies [p.84]
c.1970
100 x 100 cm
Collection the artist

93 ❦ Cotton textile with
knitting wool [p.85]
Igebu Ode, 1930-45
114.3 x 38.1 cm
Trustees of the National Museums
of Scotland, Edinburgh
(Presented by Major Gray)
(1946.966)

94 ❦ Cotton textile with
supplementary weft-floats
[pp.88-9]
Igbo, Akwete, early 20th century
170 x 73 cm
Trustees of the British Museum,
Beving Collection (1934 3-7. 116)

95 ❦ Cotton textile with
supplementary weft-floats
including fly motif
Igbo, Akwete, early 20th century
196 x 112 cm
Trustees of the British Museum,
Mrs Webster Plass
(1956 AF27.225)

96 ❦ Cotton textile with
supplementary weft-floats [p.19]
Igbo, Akwete, c.1930s
112 x 179 cm
Fowler Museum of Cultural
History, University of California,
Los Angeles, collected by
G.I. Jones (MCH X84-3)

97 ❦ Cotton textile with
supplementary weft-float design
woven on upright broadloom in
imitation of Ewe or Ewe-style
narrow-strip weaving [p.87]
Igbo, Akwete, c.1937
213 x 119 cm
Fowler Museum of Cultural
History, University of California,
Los Angeles, collected by G.I.
Jones (MCH X84-1)

98 ❦ Narrow-strip cotton textile
imitating Ewe weaving
Southern Igbo or Niger Delta,
late 20th century
167 x 94 cm
Collection Judith Appio

99 ❦ Cotton textile with
supplementary weft-float design
Igbo, Akwete, c.1937
170 x 115.5 cm
Fowler Museum of Cultural
History, University of California,
Los Angeles, collected by
G.I. Jones (MCH X84-4)

100 ❦ Black cotton textile with
supplementary weft-float design
Igbo, Akwete, c.1960
175 x 122 cm
Trustees of the National Museums
of Scotland, Edinburgh
(1980.120)

101 ❦ Cotton textile with rayon
supplementary weft-floats
[p.86]
Igbo, Akwete, 1977
198 x 130 cm
Trustees of the National Museums
of Scotland, Edinburgh
(1978.505)

102 ❦ Machine-spun
cotton textile with viscose
supplementary weft-floats in
shape of Qur'an boards [p.91]
Ebira, acquired Okene market,
late 1960s
200 x 109 cm
Collection John and Susan Picton

103 ❦ Cotton textile with
supplementary weft-floats [p.91]
Ebira, 1976
128 x 119 cm
Trustees of the National Museums
of Scotland, Edinburgh
(1977.170)

104 ❦ Cotton textile with
supplementary weft-float motifs
Nupe, c.1930-40 [p.90]
177 x 122 cm
Collection Peter Adler

105 ❦ Cotton textile with
supplementary weft-float
camel motifs
Nupe, c.1930-40
174.5 x 122 cm
Collection Peter Adler

106 ❦ Cotton textile with
salmon pink and grey warp
stripes with embroidery
Nupe, 20th century
178 x 141 cm
Collection Peter Adler

107 ❦ 'Ancient Mother'
masquerade costume and
headdress by Lawrence Ajanaku
[p.95]
Cotton, wool and appliqué
Northern Edo, 1973
Costume 105.5 cm high,
headdress 49.5 cm high
Fowler Museum of Cultural
History, University of California,
Los Angeles, Gift of Mrs
W Thomas Davis, in memory of
W. Thomas Davis
(X76.1711 and 1716)

GHANA

108 ✤ 'Little One'
masquerade costume and
headdress by Lawrence Ajanaku
Cotton, wool and appliqué
Northern Edo, 1973
Costume 74.5 cm high,
headdress 28 cm high
Fowler Museum of Cultural
History, University of California,
Los Angeles, Gift of Mrs
W. Thomas Davis, in memory of
W. Thomas
Davis (X76-1717 and 1712)

109 ✤ 'Too Fine'
masquerade costume and
headdress by Lawrence Ajanaku
Cotton, wool and appliqué
Northern Edo, 1973
Costume 150.5 cm high,
headdress 76 cm high
Fowler Museum of Cultural
History, University of California,
Los Angeles, Gift of
Mrs W.Thomas Davis, in memory
of W.Thomas Davis
(X76.1719 and 1715)

110 ✤ Factory-woven cotton
cloth resist-dyed in indigo
North-eastern Igbo-speaking
area, for Leopard Society of
Ejagham, Efik and other peoples
of the Cross River region,
20th century [p.92]
222 x 153 cm
Collection Judith Appio

111 ✤ Factory-woven cotton
appliqué and patchwork by Okun
Akpan Abuje for memorial shrine
(ngwomo) for a deceased man of
importance [detail p.93]
Ikot Obong, Afaha Clan, Ikot
Ekpene, Anang, mid-1970s
285 x 188 cm
Collection Keith Nicklin
and Jill Salmons

CAMEROON

112 ✤ Embroidered cotton gown
[p.106]
Bamenda Province, Cameroon,
July 1960
133 x 245 cm
Collection J.R. Austin

113 ✤ Silk textile (nsaduaso) with
warp-striped pattern Oyokoman
(the lineage of the Asantehene)
and float-weave in the Adwinasa
('Fullness of Ornament') manner
[p.97]
Asante, Bonwire, late 19th century
138 x 200 cm
Collection Peter Adler

114 ✤ Cotton textile [p.98]
Asante, early 20th century
244 x 143 cm
Collection Peter Adler

115 ✤ Silk textile with alternating
warp-faced and weft-faced
striping and float-weave motifs
(nsaduaso) [p.98]
Asante, Bonwire, 20th century
286 x 161 cm
Collection Peter Adler

116 ✤ Cotton and viscose textile
[p.96]
Asante, 20th century
200 x 113 cm
Collection Marine Biras

117 ✤ Cotton textile woven
on broadloom in imitation
of Asante narrow-strip weaving
192 x 110 cm
Collection K.P., Paris

118 ✤ Silk and cotton Asante
samples
Collected by R.S. Rattray (see
Religion and Art in Ashanti 1927)
Trustees of the British Museum

119 ✤ Hand-printed adinkra cloth,
black on black velour
Asante, c.1930
210 x 158 cm
Collection Afrograph

120 ✤ Cotton textile with
alternating warp-faced and
weft-faced plain weave and
supplementary weft floats
(adanudo) [pp.4 and 100]
Ewe, Kpetoe, early 20th century
316 x 180 cm
Collection Peter Adler

121 ✤ Cotton textile with
alternating warp-faced and
weft-faced plain weave and
supplementary weft floats
(adanudo)
Ewe, Kpetoe, early 20th century
280 x 169 cm
Collection Peter Adler

122 ✤ Cotton textile with
alternating warp-faced and
weft-faced plain weave and
supplementary weft floats
(adanudo)
Ewe, Kpetoe, early 20th century
182 x 90 cm
Collection Peter Adler

123 ✤ Cotton textile with
alternating warp-faced and
weft-faced plain weave and
supplementary weft floats
(adanudo) [p.99]
Ewe, Kpetoe, early 20th century
296 x 175 cm
Collection Peter Adler

124 ✤ Cotton textile with
alternating warp-faced and
weft-faced plain weave and
supplementary weft floats
(adanudo) [p.102]
305 x 180 cm
Ewe, Kpetoe, early 20th century
Collection Peter Adler

125 ✤ Cotton textile with
alternating warp-faced and
weft-faced plain weave and
supplementary weft floats
(adanudo)
282 x 176 cm
Ewe, Kpetoe, early 20th century
Collection Peter Adler

126 ✤ Cotton textile with
alternating warp-faced and
weft-faced plain weave and
supplementary weft floats
(adanudo) [p.101]
Ewe, Kpetoe, early 20th century
327 x 194 cm
Collection Peter Adler

127 ✤ Cotton textile with
alternating warp-faced and
weft-faced plain weave and
supplementary weft floats
(adanudo) [p.103]
Ewe, Kpetoe, early 20th century
270 x 180 cm
Collection Peter Adler

128 ✤ Rayon and cotton textile
(adanudo) with figurative
supplementary weft floats
Ewe, 1959
193 x 98 cm
Collection Afrograph

129 ✤ Cotton factory-woven
textile imitating something of the
style of Asante and Ewe weaving
Spintex, c.1993
142 x 100 cm
Private collection

130 ✤ Flag, imported cotton
appliqué for a military company
(asafo) with devil image [p.104]
Fante, c.1900
108 x 159 cm
Collection Peter Adler

131 ✤ Flag, imported cotton
appliqué for a military company
(asafo) [p.105]
Fante, c.1920
Proverb associated with dragon
may be 'Will you fly or will you
vanish? Either way you can't
escape us'
97 x 156 cm
Collection Peter Adler

132 ✤ Flag, imported cotton
appliqué for a military company
(asafo)
Fante, c.1940
97 x 162 cm
Collection Peter Adler

133 ✤ Flag, imported cotton
appliqué for a military company
(asafo) [p.104]
Fante, c.1950
Proverb: 'Fish grow fat for the
benefit of the crocodile (who
rules the river)'
98 x 162 cm
Collection Peter Adler

134 ✤ Flag, imported cotton
appliqué for a military company
(asafo), sewn by Kweku Kakanu,
Ekumpauanu, Kyirem No.1 Co.
[p.105]
Fante, c.1957
Proverb: 'Will you fly or will you
vanish? Either way you can't
escape us'
110 x 171 cm
Fowler Museum of Cultural
History, University of California,
Los Angeles (X81.1643)

135 ✤ Flag, imported cotton
appliqué and embroidery for a
military company (asafo), sewn by
Kobina Badowah, Lowtown, No.2
Co., 'Ghana, Independence,
Freedom'
Fante, 1981
113.3 x 178.5 cm
Fowler Museum of Cultural
History, University of California,
Los Angeles (X86.1251)

EAST AFRICA

136 ✤ Design for kanga
by Fatma Abdullah,
gouache and ink on paper
1984
56.5 x 37 cm
Collection Julia Hilger, courtesy
the family of Fatma Abdullah

137 ✤ Cotton kanga, 'Tujitahidi
Kulima Njaa isitufisidi' ('Let's
try to harvest so that hunger does
not harm/kill us') [p.108]
Bizanje EUDK, ASP, Zanzibar,
1950s-1960s
113 x 152 cm
Collection Barbara Gunnell

138 ✤ Cotton kanga, 'Maziwa ya
mama ni tamu' ('Mothers' milk is
sweet') [p.109]
Printed by Rivatex, Eldoret,
Kenya, c.1960
115 x 145 cm
Collection Barbara Gunnell

139 ✿ Cotton *kanga*, *'Usitupe chakukamata ukatumai cha kutafuta'* ('A bird in the hand is worth two in the bush') [*p.108*]
A.H. Virjee & Co., Yagi Erde 4
H.G. Peera, 1970s, acquired Zanzibar, 1994
110 x 150 cm
Collection Julia Hilger

140 ✿ Cotton *kanga* designed by Fatma Abdullah, *'Ashante Gari Ya Muhishimawa Wete'* ('Hurrah to the car of the President') [*p.109*]
Printed by Atlas, India, for export to East Africa, 1980s
107 x 157 cm
Collection Julia Hilger

141 ✿ Cotton *kanga*, *Kitsutu* design [*p.107*]
Printed by Rivatex, Eldoret, Kenya 1995
110 x 165cm
Collection Julia Hilger

142 ✿ Sample book *LKM 27 (259) Java 1846-48* with earliest items labelled for export to the Guinea coast [*p.24*]
41 x 32 cm
Collection Vlisco bv, Helmond, The Netherlands

143 ✿ Sample book *LKM (274) Stalen foor Afrika, Slendangs 1884- 1900* [*p.29*]
44 x 30 cm
Collection Vlisco bv, Helmond, The Netherlands

144 ✿ Sample book *HKM Stalenboek 1* with orders from Glasgow, 1904-6 [*p.25*]
34 x 43 cm
Collection Vlisco bv, Helmond, The Netherlands

145 ✿ Sample book *Firma Erven Ankersmit Geweven Stoffen en Technieken Sarongs, Kains etc.* with samples of woven textiles made in attempt to imitate narrow-strip cloth *c.*1912
42 x 28 cm
Collection Vlisco bv, Helmond, The Netherlands

146 ✿ Samples of cloth woven in The Netherlands by Diddens and Van Asten for sale in East and West Africa, 1920s
Gemeentemuseum Helmond, The Netherlands

147 ✿ Sample book *Broad Oak D73-D6027* with first evidence of wax print production 1909
45 x 30 cm
Collection A. Brunnschweiler & Co., Hyde

148 ✿ Sample book *United Africa Company Fancy Prints, Newton Bank*, with sample of 'Nana Prempeh' design, 1929 [*p.29*]
37 x 28 cm
Collection A. Brunnschweiler & Co., Hyde

149 ✿ Sample book *Old Ashton Fancy Designs* with sample of design commemorating the pre-colonial political figure Kojo Thompson, 1930s
38 cm high
Collection A. Brunnschweiler & Co., Hyde

150 ✿ Sample book *Newton Bank Vol XIII, late 1930s* with sample of 'Postal' design
Collection A. Brunnschweiler & Co., Hyde

Fancy print cotton textile
'Enseignement du Premier Degré' (Primary Education) design
Burkina Faso, acquired 1982
The Newark Museum, New Jersey
[*no.194*]

151 ✺ Wax print cotton textile, 'Hands and Fingers', brown hand on blue, probably printed in The Netherlands for E. Brown Flemming, Glasgow, early 20th century, label suggests design registered 1895
85 x 92 cm
Collection A. Brunnschweiler & Co., Hyde

152 ✺ Wax print cotton textile, probable original printing by Haarlem Cotton Company of 'Hands and Fingers' design, c.1904-5
[p.27]
120 x 89 cm
Collection A. Brunnschweiler & Co., Hyde

153 ✺ Wax print cotton textile, fingers with central stripe, printed by the Haarlem Cotton Company for E.Brown Flemming, Glasgow, 1905
93 x 89 cm
Collection A. Brunnschweiler & Co., Hyde

154 ✺ Wax print cotton textile, 'Hands and Fingers' with gold coins [p.27]
Possibly by Haarlem Cotton Company, c.1905
48 x 90 cm
Collection A. Brunnschweiler & Co., Hyde

155 ✺ Wax print cotton textile, 'Sword of Kingship' [p.117]
Haarlem Cotton Company for E. Brown Flemming, Glasgow, in production by 1904
98 x 90 cm
Collection A. Brunnschweiler & Co., Hyde

156 ✺ Wax print cotton textile, 'Postal' design featuring stamps for ports of colonial Gold Coast [p.119]
Haarlem Cotton Company for E. Brown Flemming, Glasgow, in production by 1905
340 x 122 cm
Collection A. Brunnschweiler & Co., Hyde

157 ✺ Wax print cotton textile, 'The Lamp' [p.117]
Engraved and printed by Haarlem Cotton Company for E. Brown Flemming, Glasgow, early 20th century
88 x 90 cm
Collection A. Brunnschweiler & Co., Hyde

158 ✺ Wax print cotton textile, Dutch landscape(?) with bridge [p.28]
Probable Haarlem Cotton Company design for E. Brown Flemming, Glasgow, 1904
Sent for registration 1912, did not go into production, design rejected in Africa
87 x 88 cm
Collection A. Brunnschweiler & Co., Hyde

159 ✺ Wax print cotton textile, Dutch landscape(?)
Probable Haarlem Cotton Company design
87 x 81 cm
Collection A. Brunnschweiler & Co., Hyde

160 ✺ Wax print cotton textile, 'The Mummy' [p.28]
Early printing by Haarlem Cotton Company for E. Brown Flemming, Glasgow, sent for registration 1912, design of limited popularity in West Africa
136 x 90 cm
Collection A. Brunnschweiler & Co., Hyde

161 ✺ Wax print cotton textile, 'Alphabet' [p.121]
Probable Haarlem Cotton Company design for E. Brown Flemming, Glasgow, in production, early 20th century
84 x 90 cm
Collection A. Brunnschweiler & Co., Hyde
This and designs 152, 155, 162-9 are of continuing popularity

162 ✺ Wax print cotton textile, 'Sunray'
Probably printed in the Netherlands for E. Brown Flemming, Glasgow, early 20th century
99 x 120 cm
Collection A. Brunnschweiler & Co., Hyde

163 ✺ Wax print cotton textile, 'Staircase' [p.121]
Probable Haarlem Cotton Company design for E. Brown Flemming, Glasgow, early 20th century
88 x 120 cm
Collection A. Brunnschweiler & Co., Hyde

164 ✺ Wax print cotton textile, 'New Fine Trail'
Probably printed in the Netherlands for E. Brown Flemming, Glasgow, early 20th century
43 x 90 cm
Collection A. Brunnschweiler & Co., Hyde

165 ✺ Wax print cotton textile, 'Sixteen Objects'
Probably printed in the Netherlands for E. Brown Flemming, Glasgow, early 20th century
90 x 90 cm
Collection A. Brunnschweiler & Co., Hyde

166 ✺ Wax print cotton textile, 'Night and Day'
Probably printed in the Netherlands for E. Brown Flemming, Glasgow, early 20th century
Each 90 x 90 cm
Collection A. Brunnschweiler & Co., Hyde

167 ✺ Wax print cotton textile, 'Banana Border'
Probably printed in the Netherlands for E. Brown Flemming, Glasgow, early 20th century
91 x 119 cm
Collection A. Brunnschweiler & Co., Hyde

168 ✺ Wax print cotton textile, 'Canoe Prow'
Probably printed in the Netherlands for E. Brown Flemming, Glasgow, early 20th century
90 x 90 cm
Collection A. Brunnschweiler & Co., Hyde

169 ✺ Wax print cotton textile, 'Sibi Saba' [p.26]
Probably printed in the Netherlands for E. Brown Flemming, samples from 1912, example illustrated, c.1925 Glasgow, early 20th century
90 x 86 cm
Collection A. Brunnschweiler & Co., Hyde

170 ✺ Fancy print cotton textile, commemorative design, 'Nana Prempeh' the Asantehene [p.118]
Printed at Newton Bank Works by the United Africa Company, c.1929
125 x 67 cm
Collection Brian Anderton

171 ✺ Green ground printed textile, commemorative design, 'Old Red Face' with portrait of George III, 1930s
Printed by James Black/S.Schwabe (Calico Printers Association) for United Africa Company, out of production for fifty years
126 x 115 cm
Collection Brian Anderton

172 ✺ Fancy print cotton textile, commemorative design, Wesley and Methodist Mission Registered and produced Basel, 1935
203.2 x 113 cm
Collection Afrograph

173 ✺ Green ground cotton textile, commemorative design, drawn and originally engraved for Coronation of Edward VIII (1937) and altered to a likeness of George VI after the abdication Design produced by Grafton African and printed by three different Calico Printers Association printworks: Broad Oak (1937-60), Buckton Value Works (1960-6) and Newton Bank Works (after 1966)
182 x 120 cm
Collection Brian Anderton

174 ✺ Fancy print cotton textile, commemorative design, Coronation 1937 and life story of King George VI [p.120]
Printed at Rhodes Works (Calico Printers Association) by S.Schwabe & Co. probably for United Africa Company, early 20th century
118 x 80 cm
Collection Brian Anderton

175 ✺ Cotton textile, one colour discharge print, commemorative design, 1935 Silver Jubilee of George V's accession
Probably printed at Newton Bank Works, Hyde, c.1950
120 x 87 cm
Collection Brian Anderton

176 ✺ Fancy print cotton textile, imitation kente narrow-strip cloth with Ghanaian flag
Acquired Ghana, c.1957
272 x 119.4 cm
Collection Afrograph

177 ✺ Fancy print cotton textile, commemorative design, Chief Obafemi Awolowo, Premier of Western Nigeria before Independence, 1957
Printed at Newton Bank Works, Hyde
63 x 116 cm
Collection Brian Anderton

178 ✺ Fancy print cotton textile, commemorative design, Independence Nigeria, 1960
113 x 592 cm
The Museum for Textiles, Toronto, Canada (T90.0410)

179 ❧ Fancy print cotton textile with photographic engraving, commemorative design, Congo Independance (30 June 1960) and King Baudouin with Patrice Lumumba in background
Printed at Newton Bank Works, Hyde, probably for Elson & Neill
107 x 118 cm
Collection Brian Anderton

180 ❧ Wax print cotton textile, commemorative design, President Senghor and Senegalese Independence [p.127]
Printed by Newton Bank Works for Grafton African, c.1960
115 x 86 cm
Collection Brian Anderton

181 ❧ Wax print cotton textile, 'Guinness gives you power'
Printed by Newton Bank Works for Grafton African, c.1960
117 x 89 cm
Collection Brian Anderton

182 ❧ Fancy print cotton textile, commemorative cloth, President Nkrumah, acquired Ghana, c.1960
203.2 x 113 cm
Collection Afrograph

183 ❧ Wax print cotton textile, commemorative design, University of Nigeria
Printed at Newton Bank Works for Elson & Neill who sold the design to A. Brunnschweiler (Nigeria), c.1961
117 x 90 cm
Collection Brian Anderton

184 ❧ Wax print cotton textile, commemorative design, Kenya Independence and President Kenyatta
Printed at Newton Bank Works, Hyde c.1963
83 x 116 cm
Collection Brian Anderton

185 ❧ Fancy print cotton textile, Pompidou and Eyadema, 'Amitié Franco-Togolaise'
Togo, 1973
116 x 78.5 cm
The Museum for Textiles, Toronto, Canada (T90.0381)

186 ❧ Fancy and screen print cotton textile, commemorative design, Amilcar Cabral and Independence, Guinea Bissau [p.140]
ICODI, Abidjan, Ivory Coast, c.1974
119 x 159 cm
The Museum for Textiles, Toronto, Canada (T90.0378)

187 ❧ Wax print cotton textile, commemorative design, 2nd World Black and African Festival of Arts and Culture (FESTAC), Lagos, 1977, 16th-century ivory mask, Benin, as emblem [p.123]
Printed by Newton Bank Works for A. Brunnschweiler & Co., Hyde and sold to SGGG Togo in transit to Nigeria
118 x 165 cm
Collection Brian Anderton

188 ❧ Fancy print cotton cloth, pale and dark blue, imitating hand-made, tie-dyed cloth
Lebanon street market, Ibadan, Nigeria, 1977
187 x 107 cm
Trustees of the National Museums of Scotland, Edinburgh (1978.506)

189 ❧ Screen print cotton textile, 19th Anniversary of Senegalese Independence 1979
Senegal
113.5 x 89.5 cm
The Museum for Textiles, Toronto, Canada (T90.0409)

190 ❧ Fancy print cotton textile, imitation patchwork design with scene of Franco/Senegalese confrontation
Sotiba, Senegal, 1980
117 x 183 cm
The Museum for Textiles, Toronto, Canada (T90.0401)

191 ❧ Fancy print cotton textile, Mosque at Touba
Senegal, c.1980
114 x 61.5 cm
The Museum for Textiles, Toronto, Canada (T90.0419)

192 ❧ Fancy print cotton textile, 'Je brûle pour vous' ('I burn for you')
Mali, 1980s
180.4 x 115.6 cm
The Newark Museum, New Jersey, Gift of George F. Taylor II and Beth Ann Taylor (84.48)

193 ❧ Fancy print cotton textile, 'Ce que femme veut' ('What women want') [p.128]
Ivory Coast, 1980s
116.8 x 180.3 cm
The Newark Museum, New Jersey (88.112)

194 ❧ Fancy print cotton textile, 'Enseignement du Premier Degré' ('Primary Education') [p.137]
Burkina Faso, acquired 1982
176.5 x 116.8 cm
The Newark Museum, New Jersey, (82.64)

195 ❧ Fancy print cotton textile, commemorative design, Agadez Youth Festival
Niger, 1982
119.4 x 113.6 cm
The Newark Museum, New Jersey, Gift of Ms Amy Greene (83.114)

196 ❧ Screen print cotton textile, commemorative design, President Nkrumah - Jerry Rawlings, Take-over, 13 December 1982
117 x 90 cm
The Museum for Textiles, Toronto, Canada (T90.0395)

197 ❧ Screen print cotton textile, commemorative design, Marcus Garvey
Printed by Sotiba, Senegal, 1987
52 x 84 cm
The Museum for Textiles, Toronto, Canada (T91.0002)

198 ❧ Fancy print cotton textile, 'Faso Tours' [p.125]
Burkina Faso, c.1987
119.3 x 177.8 cm
The Newark Museum, New Jersey (88.14)

199 ❧ Wax print cotton textile, commemorative design, Nelson Mandela, c.1987
Design produced by the Manchester merchant Logan Muckelt
Printed at Newton Bank Works, Hyde
92 x 118 cm
Collection Brian Anderton

200 ❧ Wax print cotton textile, imitation of 1935 Silver Jubilee adire [p.122]
Printed by Uniwax, Ivory Coast
Acquired Adjamé market, Abidjan, Ivory Coast, 1989
114 x 180 cm
Collection K. Bickford

201 ❧ Fancy print cotton textile, 'Si tu sors je sors' ('If you go out, I go out')
Printed at Gonfreville factory, Ivory Coast, acquired Abidjan, 1989
114 x 178.5 cm
Collection K. Bickford

202 ❧ Wax print imitation adinkra textile in black and gold [p.122]
Acquired c.1989
548.7 x 122 cm
Collection Afrograph

203 ❧ Fancy print cotton textile, 'Gold Bars and Notes' [p.128]
ITEMA, Bamako, Mali, 1980s
118 x 178 cm
Collection ITEMA, Mali

204 Q Fancy print cotton textile, 'Si je savais' ('If I'd known') [p.126]
ITEMA, Bamako, Mali, 1980s
114 x 90 cm
Collection ITEMA, Mali

205 ❧ Factory print cotton textile, 'Shared Goals', 'Parcs de Vaccination du Bétail/Partition des Terres'
Printed by Sotiba, Senegal, acquired 1990
117.5 x 243.5 cm
Museum for Textiles, Toronto, Canada (T90.0399)

206 ❧ Fancy print cotton textile, 'Cooling Fans' [p.124]
Printed by Faso Fani, Burkina Faso, 1990s
116.8 x 180.3 cm
The Newark Museum, New Jersey (95.26.27)

207 ❧ Wax print cotton textile, 'Flashlights'
Burkina Faso, 1990s [p.2]
113 x 180.3 cm
The Newark Museum, New Jersey (95.26.29)

208 ❧ Fancy print cotton textile, imitation patchwork with 'Mari Capable' ('Husband is capable') design
Printed by Utexi, Ivory Coast, acquired Adjamé market, Abidjan, Ivory Coast, 1991
114 x 181 cm
Collection K. Bickford

209 ❧ Factory print cotton textile, 'Jesus Christ, Map of Africa'.
Acquired 1991
175 x 118 cm
The Museum for Textiles, Toronto, Canada (T91.0040)

210 ❧ Fancy print cotton textile, 'La Mort est Pénible' ('Death is hard') [p.126]
Printed by Utexi, Ivory Coast, acquired Bouaké market, Abidjan, Ivory Coast, 1992
114 x 183 cm
Collection K. Bickford

211 ❧ Wax print cotton textile, 'Children are better than money' [p.126]
Printed at Nichem, Nigeria, acquired Bouaké market, Ivory Coast, 1992
114 x 180 cm
Collection K. Bickford

212 ❧ Fancy print cotton textile, patchwork design including imitation narrow-strip cloth
Printed at Utexi factory and acquired Ivory Coast 1992
114 x 179 cm
Collection K. Bickford

Fancy and screen print cotton textile
Commemorative design
Amilcar Cabral and Independence
Guinea Bissau
ICODI, Abidjan, Ivory Coast
c.1974
The Museum for Textiles
Toronto, Canada
[no.186]

213 🖎 Fancy print cotton textile,
'Hands and Fingers' [cover]
Acquired Ghana, 1993
113 x 180 cm
Private collection

214 🖎 Fancy print cotton textile,
'Fish'
Mali, 1993
160 x 112 cm
Private collection

215 🖎 Fancy print cotton textile,
'Owu Se Fie' ('Death spoils
the family') [p.126]
Acquired Ghana, 1994
115 x 345 cm
Collection John and Susan Picton

216 🖎 Fancy print cotton textile,
Nelson Mandela, for ANC
campaign in first democratic
election, South Africa 1994
[p.127]
Nkosi
120 x 165 cm
Private collection

217 🖎 Fancy print cotton textile,
commemorative design,
ANC, South Africa
c.1994
264 x 119 cm
Fowler Museum of Cultural
History, University of California,
Los Angeles (X94.26.13)

218 🖎 Fancy print cotton textile,
commemorative design,
National Party, South Africa
c.1994
181 x 116 cm
Fowler Museum of Cultural
History, University of California,
Los Angeles (X94.26.14)

219 🖎 Imitation adinkra
fancy print textile
Ivory Coast, 1994, acquired
Shepherd's Bush, London
183.5 x 114 cm
Collection Afrograph

220 🖎 Fancy print cotton textile
with map of Africa
Whitex Java, Malawi, acquired
1994 [p.10]
196 x 114 cm
Private collection

221 🖎 Fancy print cotton textile,
'Devaluation'
Printed by Faso Fani, Burkina
Faso, acquired 1995
180 x 119 cm
The Newark Museum, New
Jersey, The Members' Fund
Purchase
(95.26.40)

222 🖎 Wax print cotton textile,
'Vroom, Vroom' [p.125]
Akosombo Textiles Ltd, Ghana,
acquired 1995
117 x 544 cm
Collection John and Susan Picton

223 🖎 Fancy print cotton textile,
'Obra Tese Nkosua' ('Hand
and Egg') [p.31]
Guaranteed African Print, Nigeria,
acquired 1995
540 x 115 cm
Collection John and Susan Picton

224 🖎 Fancy print cotton textile,
'Chandeliers and Electric Light
Bulbs' [p.42]
Afprint, Nigeria, 1995
113 x 540 cm
Courtesy Afprint

225 🖎 Fancy print cotton textile,
hands with playing card motifs
and dominoes
Afprint, Nigeria, 1995
116.6 x 441.5 cm
Collection Afprint

226 🖎 Fancy print cotton textile,
'Bon Appetit'
Printed by Faso Fani, Burkina
Faso, acquired 1995
188 x 117 cm
The Newark Museum, New
Jersey, The Members' Fund
Purchase (95.26.39)

227 🖎 Wax print cotton textile,
'Six Bottles'
Printed by Vlisco, 1995
120.8 x 93 cm
Collection Vlisco bv,
The Netherlands

228 🖎 Wax print cotton textile,
'Shoes and Coil'
Printed by Vlisco, 1995
120.2 x 91.5 cm
Collection Vlisco bv,
The Netherlands

229 🖎 How does a girl like you,
get to be a girl like you?
Installation by Yinka Shonibare
Three costumes made of wax
print cotton textiles [p.141]
each 169cm high, 1995
Tailored by Sian Lewis
Made with the assistance of
A. Brunnschweiler & Co., Hyde

How Does a Girl Like You,
Get to be a Girl Like You?
by Yinka Shonibare
Installation
Three costumes of
wax print cotton textiles
Tailored by Sian Lewis
Made with the assistance of
A. Brunnschweiler & Co.
Hyde

BARCLAYS

Ghana • Kenya

Zimbabwe • Zambia

As part of a major British bank with
an established presence in thirteen African countries,
it is our pleasure to sponsor
The Art of African Textiles : Technology, Tradition and Lurex.
We are delighted to support the presentation
of one artform from Africa which has influenced
textile design internationally and which will, we hope,
fire your imaginations and perhaps lead you to Africa,
where we would be happy to welcome you.

LENDERS

Trustees of the British Museum, London

Etnografiska Museet, Gothenburg, Sweden

Fowler Museum of Cultural History, University of California,
  Los Angeles, USA

Gemeente Museum, Helmond, The Netherlands

Horniman Public Museum and Public Park Trust, London

Musée de l'Homme, Paris, France

The Museum for Textiles, Toronto, Canada

Trustees of the National Museums of Scotland, Edinburgh

The Newark Museum, New Jersey, USA

Ramses Wissa Wassef Art Centre, Egypt

Standard Bank Collection, University of the Witwatersrand,
  Johannesburg, South Africa

Peter Adler

Afprint, Nigeria

Afrograph

Brian Anderton

Judith Appio

J.R.Austin

Chant Avedissian

Kathleen Bickford

Marine Biras

Carol Brown

Arthur Brunnschweiler & Co., Hyde, Cheshire

Khamis Chehata

Clementine Deliss

Aissa Dionne

Pauline Duponchel

Jocelyn Etienne-Nugue

Barbara Gunnell

David Heathcote

Julia Hilger

Industrie Textile du Mali (ITEMA), Bamako, Mali

George Jackson

Alfousseini Kelly

Sandra Kriel

Grace Kwami

Nadine and Raoul Lehuard

Amiena Luiz

Manufactures Sénégalaises des Arts Décoratifs, Thiès, Senegal

Keith Nicklin and Jill Salmons

Nigerian Fabrics and Fashions, Brooklyn, New York
  and Ile-Oluji, Nigeria

Nike Olaniyi-Davies

K.P., Paris

John and Susan Picton

Elisha Renne

Eric Robertson, New York

Yinka Shonibare

Alec and Helen Travers

Vlisco bv, Helmond, The Netherlands

First published in Great Britain by Barbican Art Gallery
in association with Lund Humphries Publishers Ltd,
Park House, 1 Russell Gardens, London NW11 9NN
on the occasion of the exhibition
The Art of African Textiles : Technology, Tradition and Lurex
21 September – 10 December 1995
Barbican Art Gallery
Barbican Centre
London EC2Y 8DS

British Library Cataloguing in Publication Data:
a catalogue record of this book is available
from the British Library

ISBN 0 85331 682 1

Exhibition selected by John Picton and Carol Brown
and organised by Barbican Art Gallery:
Carol Brown
Lucy Brettell

Exhibition designed by Joe Casely-Hayford

Catalogue edited by
Carol Brown, Barbican Art Gallery and
Lucy Myers, Lund Humphries

Printed in Belgium by Snoeck Ducaju & Zoon NV,
Ghent

Page output by Nene Phototypesetters Ltd,
Northampton

Catalogue layout and typography
by Richard Hollis

Photographs in the catalogue by
Peter Adler: pp.22(top), 77, 97-9, 101-3
Kathleen Bickford: p.116
Jean Borgatti: p.94
Trustees of the British Museum, London: pp.66 (top), 88-9
Carol Brown: pp.21, 70 (bottom left)
Jean Brundrit: pp.48, 49, 110-13
Craftspace Touring, Birmingham: p.41
Crispin Ellis: pp.44, 45
Etnografiska Museet, Gothenburg: p.57
William Fagg: p.18
Fowler Museum of Cultural History, University of California,
Los Angeles: pp.19, 87, 95, 105 (bottom)
Jackie Guille: p.52
Béatrice Hatala: pp.35, 37, 62-3, 65, 68, 80, 96
David Heathcote: pp.38, 39
Horniman Public Museum and Public Park Trust, London:
pp.67, 69 (bottom)
Johannesburg Art Gallery p.53
Sandra Kriel: p.115
Elizabeth Laget: p.69 (right)
Lamba Sarl: p.47
Robert Lifson: pp.122 (top), 126 (top right, bottom left)
Manufactures Sénégalaises des Arts Décoratifs, Thiès,
Senegal: p.34
Musée de l'Homme, Paris: pp.62-3
The Museum for Textiles, Toronto: p.140
Trustees of the National Museums of Scotland: pp.78, 79 (top
right), 85-6, 91 (bottom)
Dennis Nervig: pp.19, 87, 95, 105 (bottom)
Newark Museum, New Jersey: pp.2, 124, 125 (top), 137
Keith Nicklin and Jill Salmons: p.93 (top)
Nigerian Fabrics and Fashions, Brooklyn, New York: p.15
John Picton: pp.8, 9, 11 (top), 12, 13, 16 (centre), 17, 23, 24,
25, 28-9, 69 (top), 121 (bottom), 122 (bottom)
Steve Rees: pp.4, 10, 11 (bottom), 16 (top and bottom), 26,
27, 31, 42, 58, 59, 61, 64, 66 (bottom), 70 (top left and right,
bottom right), 71-6, 79 (top left, bottom left and right), 81-3,
90, 91 (top), 92, 93 (bottom), 100, 104, 105 (top), 106-9, 114,
117-20, 121 (top), 123, 125 (bottom), 126 (top left, bottom
right), 127-9, 141
Mike Roberts, Electra Studios: p.84
Eric Robertson Gallery, New York: p.14
Doran Ross: p.22 (bottom)
Brian Russell: p.40
Prem Singh: p.41
Svenska Missionsförbundet, The Mission Covenant and
Church of Sweden: p.56
University of the Witwatersrand: pp.48, 49, 110-13
Sarah Wells: pp.2, 124, 125 (top), 133
Werner Forman Archive, Ramses Wissa Wassef Art Centre,
Egypt: p.60

Maps on pp. 20 and 32
by Chapman Bounford & Associates,
London

africa95